SUBALTERN MORALITY:
A POSTMODERN VISION

SUBALTERN MORALITY:
A POSTMODERN VISION

By
Ramesh Chandra Sinha

PARTRIDGE

To order additional copies of this book, contact
Partridge India
000 800 10062 62
orders.india@partridgepublishing.com

www.partridgepublishing.com/india

CONTENTS

PREFACE

This book examines the concept of subaltern morality and its post-modern vision. At the outset, I have streamlined the main features of subaltern morality. The category of subaltern is different from the category of proletariat. Proletariat is a class which emerged in the modern age. Subaltern is a category which includes race, gender and caste. The subaltern history is one thing but subaltern morality is other. The historians of Oxford University specially the subaltern studies group used the concept of subaltern for writing history. But I have used the concept of subaltern in the field of applied ethics. Oxford historians of subaltern studies group led by Prof. Ranjit Guha and Prof. Gayatri Spivak talked about subaltern history. The subaltern history is writing history from below. The subaltern morality makes a distinction between egalitarian morality and subaltern morality. The subaltern denotes marginalised people. It is social concept and concerned with morality of marginalised people.

I do not claim any originality. But there is modest attempt to apply logical relation of opposition of proposition stipulated by Aristotle in social context and develop morality of downtrodden people. It includes gender and feminist movement which Marxist ethics could not comprehend it within its class bound morality. I have discussed the concept of 'seemant naitikta' in several seminars in India. Its nearest expression is "subaltern morality". I have had the privilege of learning from responses and reflexions on my lectures in Indian Universities and world conferences.

I am thankful to Sri Varun Raj for suggesting me to get this book published from Patridge publication, A Penguin Random House Company, U.S.A. I thank to Princess Mar, publishing consultant who always inquired about the update. I have learnt a great deal from attending national and international seminars and conferences in India and abroad. I am grateful to Prof. S. R. Bhatt, the Chairman of Indian Council of Philosophical Research for nominating me in the Governing Body of Council. I am also thankful to Prof. Jatashankar, the President of Akhil Bhartiya Darshan Parishad for taking keen interest in the development of my ideas concerning subaltern morality. I express my thanks to all my friends and students for helping me to develop the ideas of subaltern morality.

R.C. Sinha
Professor & Head (Retd.)
Department of Philosophy
Patna University, Patna

CHAPTER - I

INTRODUCTION

I have tried to propose and develop the concept of Seemant Naitikta or subaltern morality in the backdrop of post-modern conditions of present day society. At the outset I make it clear that 'Seemant Naitikta' is Hindi expression used by me which has been accepted by teachers and students of Philosophy. The nearest expression in English is subaltern. So in this book 'Subaltern Morality' is quite expressive of the notion of 'Seemant Naitikta". I have used the term subaltern for marginalized and downtrodden people. It is wrong to say that Marxist alone can talk about subaltern. I have tried to interpret the concept of 'subaltern' in the framework of Aristotelian logic and applied it in social situation. In this way the expression subaltern morality is new one in the world of Philosophy. It has been used in the field of history but subaltern morality requires to be developed in the philosophical perspective.

In India, the term subaltern has been brought to the sphere of critical study of history by a group of thinkers referred to as the subaltern studies headed by Prof. Ranjit Guha and Gyatri Spivak of Oxford university. By and large subaltern study group comprises of Indian scholars. From 1982 onwards the subaltern collective has published several substantial volumes on South Asian History and society from a 'subaltern perspective'. Ranjit Guha proposes the following definition: –"The word subaltern' stands for the meaning as given in the concise Oxford Dictionary, that is, 'of inferior rank'. It will be used... as a name for the general attitude of subordination in South Asian Society whether this is expressed in terms of class, caste, age, gender and office or in any other way".1 He further states, that the term 'people' and 'subaltern classes' have been used synonymous in subaltern collectives. The social groups and elements included in this category represent the demographic difference between the total Indian population and all those whom we have described as the elite. The subaltern history is to rewrite history from common man's viewpoint. In other words, it is writing history from the below. I have tried to apply logical principles propounded by Aristotle in stating relation of opposition of propositions in social structure and conceived and developed 'Seemant Naitikta'. I have used it as a "seemant" which denotes marginalised people. It is a Hindi expression for all those who are on margins. The nearest term used for 'Seemant' is subltern in English. I have also considered that morality in post-modern society is not absolute but relative. Morality of subaltern people who are marginalized is different from the morality of elite class. Here Kantian concept of morality stipulated as universal principles are under circle. Subaltern morality does not subscribe to abstract Kantian morality. Morality is culture bound. It is contextual. It is concerned with day to day life of ordinary man. Out and out subaltern morality is relative to social conditions. It is a cultural category. It is new one. By new I do not mean any new philosophical concept but relating one concept to the other is also called new in philosophy.

The subaltern can be understood by clubbing together all categories of differentiation i.e. class, caste, age, gender and poor people. At one level or the other subaltern people are those who suffer oppressions. Ordinarily, the norms and values of society framed by elite class are accepted by down-trodden. The subordination marks the life of Dalits in India. After independence constitutional protection has been given to those who are dalits. Untouchables (Dalits) have kept their identity as a subordinated people in Indian Society because they get certain reservations and privileges. India is primarily a caste based society. Higher caste people have exploited the lower caste and poor people since the dawn of history. The subaltern people are disadvantaged and subordinated because of the hierarchical caste system which operates to benefit the dominant elite communities. The words of Parth Chatterjee are relevant here. "... no matter how we choose to characterize it, subaltern consciousness in the specific cultural context of Indian cannot but contain caste as a central element in its constitution."[2]

I contend that subaltern morality is concerned with the moral aspects of subordinate or deprived people. The subaltern morality postulates that marginalized communities are controlled by the dominant communities. Norms of society are framed by a group of dominant people. The term subaltern in Aristotelian logic denotes the relationship between two propositions. The proposition in subaltern to another if it is implied but does not imply. In this relationship, if the universal proposition is true then particular must be true but not vice-versa. Likewise if values are suitable for elite people in society, they are true and if it does not suit to elite class then false. So subaltern is implied but does not imply any other proposition. In this relationship, two propositions can be true together and also false together. Sub-alternation is the relation between two propositions having the same subject and the predicate but differing in quantity and not in quality. Resistance to the elite class and emancipation of subordinate class can be termed as subaltern social justice. In Indian context, the upper caste value system may be symbolised as A and marginalised caste morality as I. A stands for upper caste and I stands for subordinate caste. A implies I, but I does not imply A. If A is true, I must be true but not vice-versa. We can symbolise subaltern as I. Moral tenets are framed and established by elite class and followed by subordinate caste.

I have tried to understand the concept of subaltern social justice in the framework of thoughts of Ambedkar who is prominent thinker and leader of Indian dalit narratives. Indian social structure is complex interweaving of domination and subordination. Subalterns are prone to deconstruct the grand narratives of ruling class. Subaltern class is trying to come in the centre of power. According to traditional caste system, dalits are given subordinate position. The idioms of domination, subordination and revolt, are linked together. The social process is marked by struggle and resistance. The concept of subaltern morality is directly concerned with struggle of life of marginalised people.

In the post-modern society, the sub-altern social justice is very much in current. Moreover, feminism has also upset the entire male dominance of Indian social structure. Post-modernism is an attempt to de-construct the old social structure. In Indian context, Brahminical social system is under threat. Here by Brahminical social structure, I do not mean any particular caste like Brahmin but it denotes 'elitism' prevailing in Indian society. Dalits and women are sub-ordinate and deprived. The marginalised class can be termed as the 'other'. The 'other' is on the margin. They are struggling for their rightful place in social structure. As a matter of fact, it is said that in modernity project, the subaltern was not restive to come in the mainstream. In post-modernity project the subaltern are trying to be liberated. The western social thinkers pinpointed the concept of 'otherness'. The 'other' is part and parcel of social development. The feminist movement and dalit consciousness are chief marks of post- modern society. The 'other' is the main agenda of post-modern society. Post-modernism highlights differences. The hallmark of post-modernism is plurality. It attempts to de-construct the established social structure. It is a project relating to subaltern social justice in which dalits and women and economically deprived people form the group of subaltern. They have their own set of values different from elitist value system as relative and contextual. In the scheme of social justice, subaltern people try to get their fair share of benefits and burdens.

Man derives the whole of moral life from his inner self and social environment. By and large we use the phrase 'moral principles' for those principles which regulate our conduct towards society and moral questions for those which concern our relations with other people considered as members of the wider community to which we belong. By post-modern society, I mean liberal democratic society which is torn between two opposite and conflicting classes of liberal and conservatives. I do not prefer to use Bourgeoisie and proletariat since I believe that subaltern morality is not tied with the proletariat class. Here I have tried to liberate the term from the chain of Marxism. I contend that subaltern is not confined to Marxism. I have viewed 'alienation' as a moral problem of post-modern society since it degrades, dehumanises and demoralises human existence. The alienation uproots all values. But I contend that old values have collapsed and new values have not emerged fully in contemporary Indian society. This creates tension and moral crisis in the contemporary society. The subaltern people who are on margins have tried to demolish traditional morality but they have not successfully established new morality. But I do not see any reason to be alarmed due to erosion of traditional values. It is true that new set of values different from conventional values are emerging slowly in contemporary Indian society. In this course of changing society and life we are bound to loose some hackneyed tradition but not history. The contemporary Indian society is divided between two classes. One class is composed of elites who cling to egalitarian morality. The other class is composed of subaltern who is out to deconstruct the old values which serve the interest of elites. On the one hand, there is a group of elites who clamour for collapse of values, on the other hand, there is an army of subaltern people who are restive to wear out old values and create new values. So the conflict between egalitarian and subaltern morality is inevitable in post-modern society. The elitist continues to exploit the situation in his own interest. Common man is uprooted and struggling for relations of meaning. In the post-modern society man experiences his present situation in terms of disruption, conflict, self-destruction, meaninglessness and despair in all realms of life.

This is a fact that traditional morality serves the interest of the elite class. Morality is so contrived that by the mere process of obeying the laws, citizens are led to further the interest of those who govern them. C.E.M. Joad observes, "Morality, which is the name we give to law-abiding conduct is, therefore, a device on the part of rulers to ensure subservience and contentment on the part of their subjects."[3] Moral codes and beliefs are man depended. They are born of man's social situation. There is no 'man' in general. There are only specific men belonging to this or that specific social class. There are only specific moralities reflecting the specific utility, demands and situations of specific classes. Moral values conflict as these classes conflict. Moral codes or beliefs should not be treated as true or false, valid or invalid in themselves. They belong to a particular historical group. It was possible to speak in the name of subaltern morality or elitist morality. It is not possible to speak in the name of morality as such. To do so is to utter nothing but empty sounds. The rejection of any appeal to the abstract moral principle is the feature of subaltern morality. According to Marx, moralities are sectional, class-bound, and dependent on economic interest. Man is born into specific society which shapes his moral outlook. Morality of man cannot be understood apart from the social set up in which he lives and the place he occupies within social arrangements. A democrat has a different set of morality. An aristocrat has a different conscience from one who is subaltern. There are historically conditioned moralities. Morality is always a class morality according to Marxism. Ordinarily it justified the domination and the interest of the ruling class. In present day India oppressed class have become powerful enough. They are no more oppressed. They have been provided with constitutional protection. Earlier after independence the caste system was breaking due to rapid development of Indian society. But now dalits' are constitutionally protected. They do not opt to give up benefits of reservations.

The presupposition and the true end of morality is man. Man is potentially the only subject in a world of objects. Thus, anything that turns him into an object, subordinates him to powers outside him is immoral. The situation in which man humiliates himself is evil. I consider alienation as vice of the post-modern society. Despite the popularity of the concept of alienation in recent radical writings it seems clear that it is a concept useful to the moralist. It is a way of bringing out the disparity in contemporary post-industrial society between man's technological and scientific powers and his increasing degree of social dependence.

Alienation is the most serious and pervasive problem of human society more particularly of the post-modern society. We can talk of three kinds of alienation (a) alienation of the subaltern from his product (b) self-alienation of the subaltern in the process of production, and (c) the alienation of man from one another in social process. Alienation negates man's being. Ethically, man is the sole and ultimate standard in terms of which all else is to be judged. But the possibility of alienating man from his work, and his fellow human beings are vastly increased with the rise of money and technology as a universal medium of change. Money into which every thing can be converted makes everything saleable. It enables man to separate from himself not only his goods, the product of his work, but even his capacity to work itself, which he can now sale to another. Money lowers all values of mankind. It transforms him into a commodity. Money is the universal, self-constituting value of all things. It has, therefore, robbed the whole intrinsic values. With the use of money and the growth of money power, man's alienation becomes more acute. In present day society the subaltern labourer's alienated from their product, from the work that they sale on the labour market. Alienation in the practical 'material' life of man is reflected in man's moral life in the creation of abstract moral values. Subaltern morality does not subscribe to abstract value system.

If subaltern man is reduced to a mere function, he loses the sense of belonging, and thereby is relieved from the obligation to conform to moral standards and established values of elite society. So the mal-adjusted, alienated and subaltern man hardly cares for norms of society. Norms are framed by elite people. The morality of subaltern is different from the morality of elite group of society. The universal and eternal values are questioned in the post-modern society.

Is it a fact that morality has collapsed in post-modern society? If common man simply follows norms created by dominant people then morality serves the interest of dominant people. It is true that established values are loosing ground and the contemporary society does contribute something to this gradual erosion of accepted values. Subaltern people are deconstructing the age old values of life and also creating new values. Keeping in view this process of change and social mobility, I have contemplated subaltern morality.

In the present day society, man is alienated. Gradually he feels isolated. Poor people are loosing faith in established norms of society. The subaltern people are alienated in the process of production and distribution. Subaltern man suffers from self-estrangement and despair. Marginal man discovers that he is in hopeless condition and deprived of all his creations. The poor people mostly live with values which serve their daily need. Starving man is a man without values. In a life of anguish, values fail to get foot-hold. The subaltern are in process of deconstructing traditional values and social structures.

It is a fact that some of the old and traditional moral values are being eroded. It is also a fact that post-modern society is responsible for the collapse of eternal values of life. But let me admit that some old values have outlived its utility. New values of subaltern class are quite different from values of elite class. New values are emerging. In developing countries like India, where egalitarian morality has great stronghold. Radically new values of subaltern class are viewed with suspicion because they are incompatible with the egalitarian morality.

The concept of morality is undergoing a change. In global scenario men are today turning away from old established standards and are creating richer and fuller human ethics. To cling to old, fixed and static morality is a sort of dogmatism. Now nothing is good or bad for ever. This leads to the feeling that egalitarian morality is growing weak. The elitists view the emergence of subaltern new morality with awe because it takes away from them the security of their traditional value system.

To sum up, Post-modern society stands for the process of change. The cluster of old values are eroded and broken and people become available for new pattern of socialization and behaviour. The marginalised people show scant respect for egalitarian morality. The tradition bound abstract morality ceases to inspire people in fast changing contemporary society. It is true that privileged people are at dismal with eroding traditional values. They have failed to cope up with the changing moral values. It will take years to deconstruct the mind set and value system of egalitarian morality. It is a strange phenomenon to observe that marginalised people shun their subaltern value system and adopt the egalitarian morality in the process of social development.

References:

1. Ranjit Guha, 'Preface' in Subaltern Studies Writings on South Asian History and Society, Vol. I, (Oxford University Press, New Delhi, 1982), p. VIII.

2. Partha Chatterjee; Caste and Subaltern Consciousness in Subaltern Studies VI: Writings on South Asian History and Society, ed. Ranjit Guha (Oxford University Press, New Delhi, 1998). p. 169.

3. Joad, C.E.M. "The Future of Morals", John Westhouse, London, 1946, p. 6.

CHAPTER – II

APPLIED ETHICS

In applied ethics, the ethical principles are required to be applied to practical moral problems. It is application of principles to human situations. This 'human situation' is quite important. Subaltern morality is a new trend in applied ethics. Marginalised people are deconstructing the age old social structure. We can call it post-modern trend since subaltern morality does not believe in universal moral principles. Post-modern trend in ethics is neither analytic nor universalistic but applied. Post-modernity is against abstraction. The conception of morality is facing new challenges in the hands of post-modernists. Applied ethics provides frameworks within which practical moral problems can be solved. In recent times, there is growing awareness of the many moral, social and political issues which beset the post-modern world. There are burning problems of terrorism, poverty, social injustice and inequality. Subaltern morality is also concerned with social inequality. On the one hand, society is faced with crime and corruption; on the other hand, we find moral controversies and indifference towards subaltern people. There is an apparent lack of moral knowledge, sensitivity and moral courage. In contrast to traditional and modern ethical theories, a new subaltern morality is emerging in the twenty-first century. It is apparent from changing attitudes towards sex and various rightist movements. New problems have also been created by scientific and technological changes including the many issues of bio-ethics which focus on matters of life and living beings. As a matter of fact subaltern morality is also a new dash in the field of applied ethics. I have conceived and proposed subaltern morality which contemplates morality of marginalized people. It is not universal but relative to situation.

Post-modern philosophical problems have been evoked in twenty-first century due to moral conflicts and controversies between elites and subaltern. It also results in clash of civilizations and disruption in society. In ancient times, we find that there were agreements about matter of right and wrong conduct. Subaltern people also have a sense of commitment of doing what was considered right in particular cultural backgrounds. Traditional moral philosophers, therefore, shared many beliefs about the rightness or wrongness of particular acts. On the contrary applied philosophers concentrate on finding moral principles which would serve to resolve moral conflicts and ethical doubts. In post-modern era, there is little agreement on moral issues. The problem of moral philosophy is not so much one of justifying moral beliefs already known or assumed to be true. The problem is to work out a methodology and its application in order to solve the problem.

In modern age, the work of moral philosophers has focused more on problems of logical construction and analysis of language than on problems of application. The most dominant trend of the twentieth century philosophy has been linguistic analysis. It understands philosophizing as conceptualizing. P.F. Strawson in his book "Analysis and Metaphysics" adheres that concepts are clothed in language. So in order to understand philosophical problems, we have to analyse language. The analytic philosophers focus attention on philosophy of language. In fact, most of analytic philosophers could not address practical issues. Some of logical positivists like Ayer has questioned the efficacy of moral truth. The emotivists, for example, have taken the position that there is no such thing as moral truth. Intuitionists have argued that moral truth cannot be discovered by reasoning. Post-modernists in turn, have claimed that morality is a matter of cultural perspectives. Despite the emergence of linguistic philosophy in the mid twentieth century, there are philosophers who have proposed normative ethical theories. Some of the philosophers have questioned the distinction between meta-ethics and normative ethics. Kant argues that moral rules can be established on the basis of universal applicability and respect for persons. Utilitarians argue that the rightness or wrongness of actions is determined by the values of its consequences. Moral philosophers propound conflicting ethical theories. It has created the impression that philosophy has little to offer in the way of solutions to everyday practical problems of life. Perhaps this situation prompted philosophers working in the field of ethics to think in terms of applied ethics. I think subaltern morality is also deeply concerned to life situation and social structure. I understand the subaltern morality is post-modern problem of applied ethics.

In the early 1970s, philosophers have been addressing post-modern ethical problems. The chief characteristics of post-modernism are post-structuralism and non-rationalism. In the nineteenth and early twentieth century, philosophers concentrated on structuralism and rationalism. The post-modernism does not subscribe to logicality, centrality and rationality. Post-modern philosophers are lovers of multi-narratives instead of 'grand narratives'. The new fields of applied ethics have developed in the post-modern era of twenty-first century. In the past few years, there has been numbers of conferences, societies, journals, texts books and institutions devoted to the subject of applied ethics. Recent Indian professional philosophers have been taking keen interest in applied ethics. In post-modern age, new models have been developed to provide procedures for making practical decisions and resolving disputes. Peter Singer observes. "To an observer of moral philosophy in the twentieth century, the most striking development of the past twenty years would not be any advance in our theoretical understanding of the subject nor would it be the acceptance of particular ideas about right and wrong. It would, rather, be the revival of an entire department of the subject applied ethics."[1]

It is quite important to investigate the relation of theoretical ethics to applied ethics. We have to view this problem not only from the point of view of what philosophers have to offer to the solution of practical problems, but also from the point of view of seeing how subaltern morality itself might be improved by considering problems of application. By applied ethics, I understand the question of the applicability of a theory to solve the practical problems of human existence. Applied ethics is concerned with theory's ability to resolve practical disputes.

D.D. Raphel observes, "The best way to understand the nature of philosophy is to have some experience of doing it".[2] Ethical principles are abstract without moral practices. Philosophizing is theorizing. Ethical theorizing and the application of moral theory in practical moral judgement is not limited to moral philosophers. Even subaltern people without having philosophical background theorize about values. Subalterns can apply moral principles in his day to day life. Subaltern people may use or do use moral theories of one kind or another to justify their activities to resolve moral dilemmas of actual existence. Scientists are apt to theorize. Economists do therozie about economic structure. Scientists, economists and psychotherapists are prone to apply ethical principles in their respective fields. Even medical practitioners, business men and other professionals do apply ethical principles. Social scientists and theoreticians in other disciplines, assume the truth of one ethical theory or another without critical evaluation. Philosophers attempt to justify the theories they propose. Hindu ethics is supposed to fall within the province of religion as well as philosophy. In Hindu philosophy, ethics and religion both are inter-mixed. The term 'dharma' is expressive of this notion. Religious practitioners are apt to assume that principles expressed in their codes are true. Religious practitioners sometimes attempt to justify religious beliefs on philosophical grounds. Normally, ethics is concerned with rightness or wrongness of human conduct. Therefore, when one seeks answers, not only of what is right or wrong in particular case, but also of questions of correct principles, it seems only natural to turn to philosophy for answers.

The problems of applied ethics arise when man begins to reflect upon his or her moral practices and social structures. Indian social structure is linked with caste structure. There are two levels of caste structure. One is upper and other is lower. In lower category subaltern people are included, though the meaning of subaltern is more comprehensive. Moral philosophy questions the justification of actions or the reasons for judgements. In classical ethics, we find discussions on different standards of moral judgement. Difference of opinions are the source of philosophical reflections. This is a typical post-modern trend. Difference is the watchword of Derrida's Philosophy. Subaltern morality respects differences. It attempts to justify the values related to those who are on margins. In actual human situation it also arises when people are genuinely perplexed about what they should do or what they should not do. In their attempt to resolve a moral dilemma, they seek philosophical reasons for or against-particular moral actions. In so doing they often appear to personal codes or socially accepted norms. However, such rules or norms may also be disputed. In actual existence, there is always a sort of disagreement about the norms of behaviour. The accepted norms of subaltern morality seem to be conflicting. Some accepted norms of society may also seem inapplicable to concrete human situation. It may not be clear which judgement the rule requires. When ethical norms are in question, the next step is to move to ground realities. The ground realities of life and its prevalent practices help us to resolve moral conflicts. The ground reality is that elite class has different set of values and subaltern people have different set of values. Values are relative and culture bound. The ground reality conflict determines the range of their application. It justifies exceptions or clarify their meanings. Moral reasoning does not always proceed in this way, of course, for persons may begin by applying directly to accepted moral principles. Moral values are contextual. Moral values are not opinions. Values take shape in course of social interaction. Subaltern morality has taken shape during the course of interaction between different social groups.

Historically, moral philosophers have attempted to examine and defend ethical theories in order to guide actions. Principles enlighten moral judgements. The justification of moral action or beliefs are being done on moral theories. The major difference between popular opinions on ethics and theories is that philosophers usually try to clarify their positions and demonstrate their truth. Philosophers apply logical tools and reasoning to ascertain truth. Philosophers use logic to test moral principles. Philosophers also tend to give explicit attention to the methodology employed in their examinations of moral principles.

The theory of subaltern morality is influenced by philosophical heritage and historical background. Moral philosophers also come to their positions by analyzing the values of societies and its inherent contradiction in which they live. Moral values are product of inter-personal relationship. Values are not static. Values do change in changing circumstances. Philosophers, therefore, tend to reflect basic cultural views. Subaltern morality comprises values which are based on cultural backgrounds and social structures. Obviously every society has got its own cultural background. Subaltern morality is culture bound. Culture is cultivation of values. Values are product of social dynamics. We are expected to find Christian ethics among Christians or Hindu ethics among Hindus. Philosophies influence the beliefs of their adherents. The difference in the moral beliefs of different cultures have, in fact, led many people to believe in the general relativism of values. Post-Vedic Hindus were well aware of the cultural diversities and ethical relativity among people of different ages and regions. The dharmasastras and epics point out how the ways and customs of people of North and South India differ from each other. Customs are an important source of norms of conduct. Customary patterns of conduct are generally defined as that which has been handed down by earlier generations. The Ramayana and the Mahabharata assert that the injunctions of Vedas cannot be applicable to all people alike. Cultural relativism starts with the empirical fact of cultural diversity in moral beliefs. A belief in cultural or individual relativism, however, is not peculiar to post-modernism. It is a form of moral relativism which finds expressions in all periods of Indian history. The hierarchical caste structure of Indian society gives rise to egalitarian and subaltern value system.

The reasons which many philosophers have advanced to cut short post-modern relativism are very simple. They have argued that there must be universal and objective principles discoverable by reason otherwise moral judgements and moral controversies would not make any sense. Post-modernism explodes the myth of objectivity and universalism. It upholds that logicality leads to abstraction. Critics of post-modernity would say that there is no point in having a moral relativism, or in disputing the opinion of others, unless one had reason to suppose that opinions could be either correct or incorrect. Moral opinion is mere opinion about nothing, if there is no standard to determine the correctness or incorrectness of opinion. In the twentieth century, logical positivists and emotivists like Ayer and Stevenson have claimed that moral judgements are not logically justified. They uphold that moral judgements are simply expressions of feelings. Hence, moral judgements are not judgements at all. Critics of relativism say that standard of moral judgement must be objective. In order to judge actions as right or wrong, we must have some uniform standard of morality. Post-modernist does not subscribe to this view of logical positivists. Hindu ethics believes in plurality and not in uniformity.

Many philosophers have upheld that ultimate moral principles cannot be proved by deductive reasoning for, if they could be so proved, there would have to be still higher principles. But if there were higher moral principles, the principles being proved would not be ultimate, and the same argument applied to any higher principles. This leads us to fallacy of infinite regress. However, this argument ignores the possibility of establishing principles in other ways. For example, moral principles might be established by intuition, or by showing that the principles in question really are ultimate. According to teleological theory of morality, that a given value or set of values function as an ultimate end, and one may even try to show why it is ultimate by citing certain fact about the world, or certain characteristics of human nature. Plato argues that there is no higher principle than goodness itself because it bestows value on all other things. Hedonists have argued that when all is said and done the only reason anyone could give for thinking anything valuable is that it gives pleasure. There is no ultimate standard or principle.

The question is: What makes right action right or wrong actions wrong? Whether actions are right or wrong independent of our reasoning about them or whether they are right or wrong because they correspond to right reasoning? In the twentieth century, objectivists such as act-deontologists and intuitionist. H.H. Prichard, have argued that actions are right or wrong in and of themselves. Actions are right or wrong regardless of how anyone might reason about them. G.E. Moore also seems to agree with this view. Intuition or reasoning is thought to be a way of finding out which actions are right. But intuition or reasoning does not make them right. Butler observes, "…Any plain honest man, before he engages in any course of action, ask himself, or this I am going about right, or is it wrong or…"[3] The subaltern morality contemplates that right actions are those which serve the ends of marginalized people.

Some of the champions of applied ethics do not subscribe to objectivists' views on moral standard. Moral judgements are prescriptive in nature and not simply descriptive. They must issue from some authority, even if the authority is of reason itself. However, in many ancient and medieval accounts, the authority of reason was not limited to human reason, for the entire universe was thought to have a rational structure to which human reason is subordinate. In theological ethics, the standard of morality is determined by God's reason. God was supposed to have conferred his goodness upon man and his world. Such moral theories were ontological in the sense that being and value were understood to be correlative terms. Things have value according to their level of being in a hierarchy of nature, and things could be evil, or lack value, only by failing to actualize their potentialities, or by failing to achieve the perfection of the species to which they belong. Such reasoning has been the basis of self-realization theories offered by a number of philosophers from Plato to Aristotle and Augustine to Aquinas and Shankar to Sri Aurobindo. Many ethical theories do not have logical or ontological foundation for they are often quite relativistic. They do not presuppose a belief in essential nature or transcendental values. It does not transpire that all traditional moral philosophers are idealistic or perfectionists. Epicureans in Greece and Carvaka in India were materialists who believed that summum bonum of human existence is pleasure. There is nothing transcendental. The end of life is to seek pleasure. Pleasure is the be all and end all human existence. The standard of moral judgement is hedonism and not perfectionism. The stoics believed in a natural law based upon one's place in the universe, but they were more concerned with attaining peace of mind by controlling their feelings and sensuality. In India, Shankara and Sri Aurobindo were concerned with self-realization.

According to Platonic and neo-Platonic theory, our ability to know what is right or wrong is guaranteed by the Divine illumination of human understanding. Modern school of rationalistic philosophers such as those of Descartes, Leibnitz and Spinoza believed in innate ideas. A belief in innate ideas need not be based on faith in God. Kant claimed that there is a first principle of practical reasoning implicit in moral reasoning. Kant conceived God as secondary postulate of morality. Kant upheld that moral laws are Marxisms which can be universally applied. But the stand point of subaltern morality is different one. The standard of subaltern morality is also different. It is true that subaltern morality is teleological one. If it serves the end of downtrodden and marginalized and women then it is good otherwise it is bad. The be all and end all of subaltern morality is the well-being of marginal people.

Kant was agonistic but rationalist. He opposed empiricists. Epicureans thought that morality could be founded on human sentiments. Bentham and Mill did not deny Kant's principle of universalizability as they did amend and supplement it by arguing that moral reasoning requires a consideration of the consequences of actions, Bentham and Mill hoped to lay foundations for a science of ethics by uncovering the logic of moral reasoning. Kant believed that his moral rules applied to all human beings. Kierkegaard accepted Hegelian idea of an Absolute, but he declined to accept Hegelian rationalistic account of ethics. According to Kierkegaard, man is united with God not by reason but by choice. Marx accepted Hegelian dialectic process but he turned Hegelian dialectic process upside down.

As a matter of fact, Marx can be termed as the representative thinker of modernism. Marxism, pragmatism and existentialism are prominent philosophies of modern age. However, a new type of analytic philosophy was introduced by Russell, Moore, Wittgenstein and Strawson. Analytic ethics is concerned with the meaning of ethical terms. Traditional philosophers of ethics have been concerned with moral reasoning and language. A new distinction was drawn between meta-ethics and normative or substantial ethics. In Principia Ethica, Moore claimed that the primary question of philosophic ethics is the meaning of good, not what kind of things are good. The debates which followed during the first-half of the century were largely debates on meta-ethical questions. Moore contemplated that the meaning of good was the central question of ethics. He argued that good could not be proved by any other property. Goodness cannot be proved by any process of reasoning. That is what Moore meant by saying that goodness must be intuited, but he thought that other moral properties, such as rightness, could be derived from goodness by a process of utilitarian reasoning. Deontologists thought that rightness or obligatoriness was the fundamental moral concept. H.H. Prichard held that the rightness or wrongness of each and every particular act must be intuited. The reason is that there is no other properties which make acts right. Sir David Ross also upholds that rightness is fundamental, but he thought that moral principles, not particular instances, must be intuited, since he believed that moral rules cannot be derived from any higher principle. Thus much of the debate focused on whether good or right is the basic concept of ethics and whether particular acts could be justified by rules or principles.

Logical positivism rejected the basic assumption of intuitionism that moral terms refer to moral properties. The Logical positivist like Ayer argued that the primary function of value terms is to express human emotion and that because of this, moral utterances are neither true nor false. Logical positivists made a fundamental distinction between facts and values—between cognitive and non-cognitive statements. Jean Paul Sarte argued that moral judgements could not be determined by principles. Values are created by choice. Thus, following World War II, moral philosophy seemed to be dominated by the metaethical positions or emotivism. They restricted the place and function of reason in ethics. These views had a powerful influence upon traditional theories like Utilitarianism and Rigorism. J.J.C. Smart used emotivism to support his preference for utilitarianism. R.M. Hare combined the Sartean idea of choosing moral principles with a Kantian requirement to universalize that decision. In the 1950s and 1960s a new version of utilitarianism developed and a distinction was made between rule-utilitarianism and act-utilitarianism. Rule utilitarianism holds that an act is right if and only if it conforms to a set of rules general conformity to which would maximize utility. Rule utilitarianism tells us which rules fulfil his stated requirements. Moral rules according to intuitionist like Ross were justified by the principle of utility. Rule utilitarianism is a two-staged theory in which at the first stage, moral rules are justified by utility and, at the second stage, particular actions are justified by means of the rules.

It is appropriate to ask for reasons in ethics. Moral evaluation is not simply a matter of intuition, emotion or choice. The distinction between facts and values was also under question because it seemed that actions could be justified by social practices. Values can be derived from facts. John Rawls proposed a social contract theory, according to which principles of justice are based upon fair consent. Rawl's theory evoked interest in ethics which extended beyond philosophic circles. The development of game theory of Wittgenstein, utility theory of Mill and social welfare theory of John Rawls also added new dimension and techniques to ethical analysis. Fox and Joseph observes, "Applied philosophy is concerned with clarifying moral issues and determining how general principles can be applied to concrete cases."[4] Traditional normative ethics is abstract. Some of the issues of applied philosophy were raised. They called for classes in world peace, environmental issues, social justice and human rights. Problems of bio-ethics and professional morality also began taking interest in applied ethics. This trend has assumed enormous importance in the recent syllabus of Indian universities.

The growth of applied ethics has posed a problem to theoretical ethics. Theoretical ethics are normative in character. Neither normative ethics nor virtue ethics play effective role in solving practical problems of life. Fox and Joseph states that "Theoretical ethics also appears to be threatened by the possibility that applied ethics may continue to grow and prosper without theoretical guidance, for the issues of applied ethics are sometimes argued within the contexts of popular debate without any explicit attempt to apply theories at all. Theories are applied mechanically without any attempt to determine whether they are appropriate or inappropriate."[5] In the post-modern conditions, there is need for coupling theoretical and applied ethics. The application may prove to be a means of testing and improving theory. It may enable applied ethics to rise above mere application to the level of philosophy itself. Applied ethics has not benefited from recent developments in ethical theory. The ethical theory has not yet been improved by considering problems of application. John Stuart Mill and John Dewey address social issues. They are not consistent with post-modern ethical trends. In the modern age, philosophers have been concerned primarily with abstract issues concerning the objectivity of moral judgements. In the post-modern age ethics is relative to cultural conditions.

True that science and technology influenced our ethical world-view in the wake of modernism. Science gave the models for truth. Scientific claims are tied to observable data. The logical positivists argued that the very meaning of a proposition is dependent on verifiability or falsifiability. A.J. Ayer in his book "Language, Truth and Logic" has mentioned that ethical statements are emotive. They can't be verifiable. They are non-cognitive. Hence they are meaningless. Subaltern morality does not indulge in analysis of language. It is concerned with social dynamics and its value system. It is concerned with practical life of poor and marginalized.

Post-modern trends in applied ethics anticipate cultural relativism. They questioned universal moral principles. Post-modernists called attention to multiplicities of moral practices. Cultures have sub-groups cultures. Post-modernity envisaged plurality and differences. There are individual differences within groups. Cultural relativism contemplates that each culture or individual has opinions about what is right or wrong, but the theory provides no basis for claiming that any opinion is or even could be objectively true.

It is generally upheld that science is deterministic. Post-modern trends are in conflict with deterministic nature of science. Ethics postulates freedom of will. In other words, causal determinism conflicts with the ethical supposition of freedom and responsibility. Marxism relegated ethics to a deterministic process. It holds that ethical theory is an instrument of class exploitation. The post-modern philosophic vision of Jacques Derrida have challenged the positivist thesis that scientific knowledge is directly linked to observation. Fox and Joseph observe, "The objectivity of science seems to rest more on good reasons, the consistency of shared data and interpersonal agreement than upon uninterpreted observations."[6] The post-modern views on science have created a new climate of multiple opinions in which ethical theory can be re-evaluated and reassessed. If the theoretical interpretation of data plays an important role in science, then one may suppose that it may do so in ethics as well without any apparent loss of objectivity. Human aspiration, reason and agreement may be regarded as elements which give ethics an objective grounding. Ethical theories requires to be tested in concrete human situations.

Linguistic analysis of ethical terms has lost its charm in post-modern world. I think, mere analysis and clarifications of meaning of ethical terms are not enough. Man is not content with words and its meanings. He loves actions and applications in concrete human situation. The application of moral principles in life and society is very important. Mere analysis is abstract. The striking development in post-modern ethics is practical application of moral principles in varying human situations. Peter Singer rightly observes, "To an observer of moral philosophy in the twentieth century, the most striking development of the past twenty years would not be any advance in our theoretical understanding of the subject nor would it be the acceptance of any particular ideas about right and wrong. It would, rather, be the revival of an entire department of the subject: applied ethics."[7] I think life is larger than logic. Life needs application of logic for human well-being. Mere consistency has no meaning unless it furthers social life. The myth of universalism has been exploded in post-modern age. Relativism has become order of the socio-moral thought under the impact of post-modernism. Cultural relativism and difference cannot be brushed aside. Abstract idealistic moral principles and scientific deterministic theories which threatened the assumption of human freedom now appear to be incapable of explaining many human activities.

The demand for applied ethics has come in the post-modern society which is full of tension and disruption. The substantive ethics seems to be losing its ground and giving way to applied ethics. Post-modern philosophers are prone to do applied ethics. Some of the philosophers of post-modern age are trying to deconstruct the edifice of grand system of ethics. They are trying to resolve a variety of vital issues. Their position is that of relativist. They uphold that there is no widely accepted single theory to support their investigations. The domain of ethical theory and its methodology and its relationship to application are pluralistic and relativistic in nature.

In the modern age, the emphasis was on ethical theory. In the post-modern age, the insistence is on application of moral principles to living existence of human beings. The twentieth century having background of objectivity and analytical inclinations to determine the meaning of ethical terms have lost its glamour. It also lost continuity with changes in society and in the various sciences. It also lost much of its continuity with traditional theories. Social sciences like economics developed sophisticated models of rationality and choice independently of philosophical ethics.

Philosophical theories ignored post-modern trends and development. It appears that philosophers need to develop a sense of cultural relativism of post-modern age. "A Theory of Justice" by John Rawls published in 1971, was an exemplary attempt to construct a substantive ethical theory of justice. The theory lays down basic principles and a methodology of its application. In general the work of Rawls signaled (1) a new confidence in substantive theory; (2) reworked conceptions of objectivity and data in ethics; and (3) a view of ethical theory as a way of ordering basic conventions. Most importantly, from the standpoint of applied ethics, his theory seemed to lend itself to a wide variety of applications from medicine to business and law.

Critics may say that Rawls theory of justice appears to suffer from shortcomings. First of all, the theory is presented in a highly abstract form. This is typical of traditional ethical theories but the abstract principles of traditional theories could be given more specific interpretations because they usually reflected the social practices of their times. By contrast, Rawls defends his principles on the basis of assumptions which diverge widely from current practices. For example, he assumes full compliance with the principles he lays down, although in practice such compliance cannot be assumed. He leaves key terms undefined or inadequately defined. The questions of standard of morality is ignored. It assumed that applications takes place instantaneously. Rawls theory is not easily applied, at least as it currently stands.

In the modern times, ethical theory has not been developed with a view to application. It seems that ethical practices is not guided by theory. In economics, application has been guided by theory. Amartya Sen has tried application of ethical principles in economics in his book "Ethics and Economics". Most of applied economics is based upon similar theoretical foundations. Different schools in economics tend to use similar argumentations and economists often refer to the same basic data when defending interpretations and theories. In philosophic ethics, there has been a significant gap between theoretical ethics and applied ethics. There is little agreement about principles, the relevance of data, the appropriate methods of theory construction and testing.

The post-modern demands for the application of ethical theories prepares the ground for constructing new theories. It attempts to modify older theories in post-modern conditions. In recent past, we find that "Gandhivada" has been transformed into "Gandhigiri". The visual communication is in touch with the masses. "Gandhivada" was theoretical and idealistic but "Gandhigiri" is applied Gandhism. Though the expression is not very happy one for traditional Gandhiates but we can't evade visual media which is very powerful. I think "Gandhigiri" is post-modern expression. The term "Gandhigiri" was used by the visual media keeping in view the tone and temper of post-modern age. Similarly, the term "Netagiri" stands for true picture of present day political society. Likewise the expression "Hindutava" in place of Hinduism is post-modern expression which is laden with meaning in a changing context. These expressions indicate post-modern conditions. The post-modern ethical theories may be tested by their ability to resolve problems of existence. In modern perspective, ethical theory has potential for generating agreement based upon rational considerations, objective data, and accepted principles of action. Such ethical theory would enable persons to form basically similar patterns of approach to the solution of practical problems. In the post-modern ethical trends, internal consistency would not be sufficient. Differences, multiplicities and relativity are key concepts of post-modernity. The post-modern view is that theory may provide adequate guidance for application in the near future. In post-modern conditions, theory would be used to resolve difficult cases. It ensures consistency in application of moral principles. It provides guidance in action. It also provides relative standards of morality which can be easily applied to judge moral behaviour in day-to-day life.

But work in the fields of applied ethics cannot wait for theory to advance to the point of providing clear guidance. Indeed, theory will probably not advance unless current investigations into practical revealed areas of agreement and principles on which philosophers can rely in reconstructing their theories. It may be the case that a plurality of approaches to ethics is required. On the one hand, modern philosophy of ethics may need to continue their investigations in abstract ethical and meta-ethical theories but with the idea of application. On the other hand, application for post-modern ethicists may need to proceed without dependence on existing theory. Modern philosophers were concerned for the universality and certainty of their moral arguments. The concern of post-modern ethicists is its application. There is a remarkable shift from high level theoretical principles to practical ethics.

Applied ethics, unlike theoretical ethics, cannot ignore actual living conditions. Applied ethics is directed towards the solution of controversial issues of day to day existence. It must assume disagreement. Hence, it seeks procedures for moving from disagreement to agreement. Applied ethics, therefore, must address the question of practical life of post-modern world. However, the problems of a practitioner, such word as health care professionals, are different from those of an applied philosopher. For the practitioner faces such constraints directly, whereas the philosopher can consider how such constraints may be weakened or removed. In considering problems of application, the philosopher cannot simply assume existing or ideal states of affairs, for he must consider how actual conditions can be changed to bring about desirable results. Emphasis on actual conditions points out a need for interaction between philosophers, social scientists and practitioners in other fields.

I uphold that theoretical ethics and applied ethics are not likely to part company. Applied ethics cannot thrive at the cost of theoretical ethics. Theoretical ethics and applied ethics may perform different roles in different spheres but there is need for integration of theory and application. Theory should gain support from consensus reached on the applied level. Applied ethics should be benefited from the extension of accepted principles to controversial cases. The question boils to the point as to how moral principles can be applied in actual living condition. I think, theory prepares the background for successful application of moral principles. Fox and Joseph observe, "In general, theory needs to become more responsive to the complexities of genuine moral problems, and application needs to benefit from the general understanding, rational consistency, and coordination of judgments which ethical theory can provide."[8]

Postmodernism is a philosophical trend which helps us to understand the reality of social phenomena. The benefits of modernity were mostly cornered by the elites and the high-ups of the society. Modernity in its turn came to oppress the human kind and turned it into certain set ways of thought and actions not friendly to subaltern people who are on margins. Karl Marx is the representative thinker of modernity believes in rationality. Post modernity deconstructs modernity. The concept of subaltern is different from proletariat. The term subaltern was popularized by Italian Marixist Antonio Gramsci. But my use of "Seemant" is different from Antonio Gramsci concept of subaltern. Since I don't find appropriate word other than subaltern as nearest english version of 'Seemant'. The concept of subaltern includes class, gender, colour and caste. Proletariat denotes working class but subaltern is not confined to class. It is comprehensive concept. My use of 'Seemant' is cultural category where as subaltern is economic category. 'Seemant' is not exact Hindi translation and subaltern is not exact English translation. The word 'Seemant' is more comprehensive. My interpretation of 'seemant' is different since it includes gender and race, caste and colour. Seemant is near to Aristotelian expression of subaltern rather than Gramscian use of subaltern.

In India, modernity gives the narratives of elite classes, upper caste Hindus and the well off politicians. The emancipation of the subaltern is nowhere in sight. Modernity has in a way created grand narratives as coined by Lyotard. These grand narratives have been established as universalizing values. Communism, democracy and capitalism are glaring examples of grand narratives created by modernity to defeat the cause of subaltern who are characterized by 'culture of silence' and just standing on margins. The grand narratives have also given fundamentalism reasserting itself. There is eco-fundamentalism, academic fundamentalism and in the economic realm, there is market fundamentalism. Political fundamentalism has put their trust in grand narratives. India has established value system in such a way that the moral values created by high-caste Hindus are the only imitation models for the subaltern of the country. Institutional authorities- religious, educational, economic and developmental- have been deconstructed. It looks with skepticism all the vague notions of progress. It argues for the rejection of universalistic beliefs and abstract truths.

Applied philosophy is the present trend of philosophising. It is the guiding paradigm of Indian value system. Take for instance the values stipulated in Bhagwat Gita. This depicts the whole concept of life during the course of war. Bhagavad Gita is a part of the great Mahabharat which depicts the fierce war between Kaurav and Pandav. They constantly argue that Indian society is in a process of transformation. The massive change is 'adaptive change'. There are traditions in India which have not been changed. They still maintain their status quo. They have been partly modernized. This is how functionalism has put Indian value system into a closed cage. Still we love abstraction and universalization. Contemporary Indian philosophers have been very vocal in stressing the importance of cultural change. It stipulates change in value system, customs and manners. All this has put on the backseat the need to understand the hard realities of life which the subaltern people have to face. Concepts which have become the prime treasure of contemporary philosophy include sanskritization and caste functionalism. Elite castes and the higher ranks of society are the imitation models for the subaltern. Subaltern people follow elite class in the matters of life styles and ethics. Rules and regulation, policies and practices are set by elite of society and subaltern people follow it into practice. If the disadvantaged groups have to undergo the process of cultural change, they have to follow the values, customs, beliefs and life styles of the higher castes. In this process of the so-called cultural change there is no question for the loss of identity of subaltern. The concept of sanskritization was used first by social thinker namely M.N. Srinivas to describe the process of cultural mobility in the caste hierarchy of Indian social structure. The contribution by the eminent social thinker was given with the hope that the subaltern would transform themselves on the lines or model of the dominant caste. The value system of subaltern will change in the course of culturalization or Sanskritisation. The structure of society that India once had during the times of Vedas or the Epics or the golden period of ancient India does not exist in postmodern age. Our civilization is great one. But, values which developed through this period have ceased to cope with the passage of time. How can and do we justify our contemporary existence by clinging to the value system of ancient age. We can shun old value system and create some new values. We can not get rid of history but we can give up some outdated values.

Modernity made attempts to give a death blow to some old values of tradition. But there is a broad consensus among all contemporary philosophers on modernity that it involves a belief in the possibility of human progress and rational planning to achieve its objectives. Modernity is a belief in the superiority of rational thought compared to dogmatic religious faith and emotion. It is just trust in the ability of technology and science to solve human problems. It is a belief in the ability and rights of human beings to shape their own lives and the reliance upon manufacturing industry to improve living standards. Society developed hand in hand with modernity. It was also thought that scientific principles would be used to understand society. Rational thought could be employed to ensure to fulfill and meet human needs. Philosophers took up the theme of modernity sometime in the beginning of seventies. But, the perspectives adopted by them were erroneous. It does not analyze Indian modernity in the context of India's tradition. Indian tradition adheres hierarchical caste system and transcendence. Contemporary Indian society is dynamic and does believe in science, technology and development. But our value systems are deeply rooted in tradition.

Classical Indian Philosophers make straightjacket classification of western and Indian societies. The former being egalitarian and the latter hierarchical. Here I propose that subaltern people form major chunk of Indian society. Indian society is traditional one and the western society is modern one. Contemporary Indian thinkers are true to the civilizational depth of India. They conclude by saying that a kind of adaptive transformation is taking place in India which makes traditions to undergo process of a change. Post-modern India is very much influenced by Indian civilizations and British inspired functionalism. Post-modernism believes in multiplicities.

The euphoria of modernity has left people disenchanted. Danial Bell's famous volume, "The Cultural Contradictions of Capitalism" (1976), has presented a poignant diagnosis of ailing segments of American Society. It demonstrates successfully the dissociation of norms from values and of means from ends. Modernity suffered a credibility crisis. This crisis made suspect the ruling assumption of modernity, namely, the assumption that science, reason, and rationality would lead to the making and shaping of society. But the current development augments loss of family values and disintegration of social forms.

Some Indian thinkers contemplate that modernity and post-modernity are the co-process of development and change societies. Post-modernity symbolizes a critique of modernity as well as a new perception of the current nature of social processes and the consequent emergence of a new conception of society and social movement.

The Applied Philosophers forget that the impact of modernization is not similar on all the traditions. Therefore, to consider modernity with tradition is theoretically wrong. Ordinarily, we adhere that outdated values of tradition can be negated but we cannot reject the good aspects of tradition. We can afford to forget some of the bad aspects of tradition but we cannot negate history. Post-modernity believes in technology. Millions of our villages will get self-sufficiency. Agriculture would enable the people to fulfill their livelihood needs. It was believed that green revolution would strengthen the subaltern people. But modernization did not bring any worthwhile change in the life of subaltern people.

At the urban level, the subaltern masses have changed due to industrialization. Post-modern trends coupled with new technology are posing a challenge to modernity in India. In post-modern Indian society backward and subaltern have not liberated. Social stratification of caste and religious identities took the shape of fundamentalism. Capitalism worsened the deteriorating status of the subaltern and their value systems. Philosophers of modernity endorsed elitist value system based on hierarchical caste system. Hierarchical caste system creates gulf between upper caste and lower caste. Some Indian and western scholars tried to understand Indian value system more objectively. For example, Gandhi struggled for India's freedom and tried to improve the situation of Harijans who are untouchables due to hierarchical caste system. This attempt of Gandhi was exemplary.

Industrialization and modernity have brought some changes in social structure and Indian value system. But, by and large, the changes are not basic to the Indian value system. It appears that modernity has failed as a process of transformation. There are changes which have benefitted only the higher castes and elites. Post-modernity has thrown a challenge to modernity. It was expected that with the coming of modernity, Indian society and its value system, mainly value system of subaltern would come out of the rut and make progress. History would be forward looking. Subaltern value system will prevail over aristocratic and elitist value system. The subaltern narratives deconstruct the grand narratives of elite class.

Why is it that despite radical measures to bring about change, the norms of social hierarchy of empowerment of women and extent of religious and cultural tolerance remain confounded? Culture changes only slowly. Social philosophers have variously explained it as being a result of the fact that a culture is always integratively continued. Each culture has a basic 'theme' or 'pattern' or 'symbolic code' which constitutes its core. All changes in it are mediated by it.

The Indian society has been suffering terribly. Democracy has been abused. Development has gone in favour of the rich and well off of the society. Even modern people have lost faith in science and technology since technology dehumanizes human beings in general and subaltern in particular. Technology is not within reach of subaltern people who are poor and illiterate. The rich and affluent people have access to technology and they reap all benefits. Subaltern people have become more skeptical about the benefits of technological advancement. As a matter of fact, people have lost faith in the proclaimed political beliefs and grand narratives that claim to be able to improve society. It has been a common observation in India that only modernity-inspired rationalism cannot solve the manifold complex problems of the subaltern and down-trodden masses. Modernity loves grand narratives. It believes in system building. Post-modernity loves multi narratives. Pluralism is the watch word of post-modernity. Subaltern narratives are in a sense post-modern. Subaltern morality comprises values of downtrodden and common man.

The advocates of the idea of postmodernism claim that the classic social thinkers took their inspiration from the idea that history has a shape and structure. It goes somewhere and leads to progress. This notion has collapsed. There are no longer any 'grand narratives'. There is no general notion of progress that can be defended. There is no such thing as history in-itself. There are histories and not a history. Indian society is primarily concerned with caste narratives. Indian society has histories and not history.

Social philosophers have created a huge literature on caste narratives and its values. Hierarchical caste system is related to subaltern narratives. Castes are the oldest social formations of Indian society. These hierarchy-based divisions have not posed any challenge to the early society. They are considered to be a part of our all-enveloping religion. There are ample evidences to show that Indian value system were essentially a caste-based system and functional. Inspite of all onslaughts on the system, it persists. It is understood that Varna Vyavastha degenerated into caste system. But, with the rise of modernity in India, the society developed caste identity. Caste identity appeared for political convenience. There has been a vigorous development of caste consciousness which is called casteism in the present day society. Caste is a fact but casteism is evil of society. Casteism is disvalue. Politics plays a dangerous role to benefit from caste identity. This identity has many faces. It also has a role to play in voting behaviour, economic development and social change. In his recent work, Amartya Sen puts forward the thesis that most of current problems of India are due to the conflicting identities of the people. He deals with the problem of identities in his book "Identity and Violence". Amartya Sen diagnoses the structure of identity and says that a person has multiple identities. Philosophers argue that caste identity is cultural identity. In Indian society caste is a major determinant factor in streamlining family relation and marriage. The tendency of Philosophers has been to assess secular themes in the perspective of culture. Culture has always been related to religion, caste and fundamentalism. Amartya Sen is very specific when he clarifies the concept of identity. Our cultural identities can be extremely important, but they do not stand above and aloof from other influences on our understanding and priorities. There are a number of qualifications that have to make while acknowledging the influence of culture on human lives and actions. However, culture plays a great role in our social life. But it is not the only factor to shape our life. Other things, such as class, race, gender, profession, politics also matter. Second, culture is not homogenous. There can be great variations even within the same general cultural milieu. Culture interacts with other determinants of social perception and action. For example, economic globalization brings in not only more trade, but also more global value system. Culture cannot be seen as an isolated force independent of other influences.

In the foregoing analysis, we have tried to explain that philosophy as rational discourse has certain obligations towards the society. In the past, the mainstream philosophy has not done anything worthwhile for the improvement of Indian society. Albert Schweitzer in his book 'Indian Thought and its Development' says that Indian Philosophy is world and life negating. Its methodology has always remained conservative and concerned with ultimate goal of Moksha. As a matter of fact the ideal of 'moksha' is vacuous. It has no content. It is pure consciousness. It is transcendental. Subaltern narratives put a question mark on egalitarian morality.

The modernity which India witnessed during the last two hundred years has been a study of society as a whole. The modern perspective has not succeeded in understanding the reality of our society. Modernity has lapsed into post-modernity due to rapid change in technology. Ordinarily it is believed that post-modernity is cut off from history and tradition. It is a radical one. It advocates all sorts of anti-tradition narratives. I think post-modernity is not cut off from tradition. It is continuity of old and new values. Post-modern society is now seen as a reality devoid of centrally binding value system to be conceived of as a totality. Postmodernity in India believes in multi-narratives. It contemplates unity in difference. It is strange phenomenon that religious values are reappearing in postmodern society. Habermas considers post-modern society as post-secular society. We have tried all these perspectives to analyze the problems of our society. The traditional value system and conventional paradigm characterized by historicism has come to an end. The liberal democratic values have become prevalent in postmodern society. Postmodernism deconstructs objective value system. It adheres to relative values. It deconstructs grand narratives of modernity. It is post-structural and post-secular. It subscribes to values dear to subaltern people who have been marginalised since the inception of our civilization. I think a new turn in social, political and cultural value system is taking place. But post-modernity is back to its culture and tradition. There is harmony between culture and technology, tradition and modernity. Post-modernity may suffer severe criticisms since the age has seen some unnatural events like same sex marriages. We can decry this trend of same sex marriage but we can not deprive transgender its legitimate place in subaltern narratives. Transgenders are subaltern and they have been marginalized in the society. They need to be brought in the mainstream. The post-modern developments are neither fully cut-off from tradition nor from modernity. It is a blend of tradition and modernity. It is a passage from modernity to post-modernity. Subaltern narratives are important in the sense it focuses on those who are marginalized.

References:

1. Singer, Peter; Applied Ethics, Oxford University Press, Oxford, 1986, p. 1.
2. Raphel, D.D., Moral Philosophy, Oxford University Press, Indian edition, 1986, P. 1.
3. Butler, Joseph; Five Sermons, New York, Liberal Arts Press, 1949, p. 45.
4. Fox, Richard M. and Demarco, Joseph P; New Directions in Ethics, Routledge and Kegan Paul, New York, 1986, p. 11.
5. Ibid; p. 12.
6. Ibid; p. 14.
7. Singer, Peter; Applied Ethics, Oxford University Press, 1986, p. 1.
8. Op.cit., p. 18.

CHAPTER – III

HISTORICAL PROCESS

The "Historical Process" attempts to streamline the nature and meaning of social development. Here I contend that subaltern morality and its value system emerge in the course of historical process. In the first section, I have dealt the notion of the end of history and in the second section, I have given an outline of new social organisation and its moral values. The thesis is that development does not mean only economic development. There is a difference between development and social development. By social development, I mean the total development of human existence. This is inclusive concept which integrates both economic and cultural aspects. In this sort of inclusive development old value system gives way to new values of technological society.

Hegel conceives dialectical process as historical process. He understands that development is through dialectical process of ideas. The critics of Hegel consider dialectical process as bloodless march of categories. Hegel's historical process is the journey of ideas, Marx dubbed Hegel's historical process as an abstract one. Hegel's dialectical process of ideas is idealistic one. Marx has put the entire process as upside down and propounds materialistic historical process.

We live in the world which is changing every moment. In this changing world, what will be plausible concept of subaltern morality and social development. It is obvious that social and political scenario of the post-modern world is changing. The concept of social development can be understood within the framework of historical process. I contend that narrative of development is required to be presented in a fresh way in subaltern perspective. Many philosophers who were staunch Marxists have drifted away from Marxists ideology. Anthony Giddens observes, "Many of those who once chose to call themselves Marxists both in the East and West, have turned away sharply from such an intellectual and political affiliation. Soviet Marxism, of course, has collapsed completely, even in China a certain version of Marxism-Leninism still forms the official ruling ethos. In Western Europe and elsewhere, moreover, most parties which used to term themselves communist have now changed their official titles".[1]

In this context it will not be out of place to mention American Professor Francis Fukuyama of Japanese origin who contends in his book entitled "The End of Order" that the great disruption in social order of the present day society is obvious. The post-modernists have parted company with Marxists interpretation of historical process and declared the end of history. The end of history means here the end of ideology. Ideology means a set of values. Here in Post-modern age we are primarily concerned with teleological ideology. After the 18th century revolution, a new narrative of social and political success has been portrayed. Marx conceived the historical process as process of struggles. It is struggle against Bourgeoisie value system and its exploitation.

The nature of historical process is no more speculative and abstract one. Ordinarily, the notion of the 'end of history' as contemplated by Fukuyama is obscure. How the end of history is possible? The end of history has been understood in the sense of the end of dialectical process. The meaning of history is not confined to the stories and struggles of kings and kingdoms. It is not simply story of events. The end of history means the end of the class struggle. According to Marx, the historical process means the process of class struggle. When Francis Fukuyama talks about the end of history, he means the end of class conflicts. Fukuyama observes, "What we may be witnessing do not just the end of the cold war or the passing of particular period of postwar history, but the end of history as such that is, the end of mankind's ideological evolution and the universalisation of western liberal democracy as the final form of human government."[2]

In the end of historical process, the slavery system came to end. Subalterns are not necessarily slaves. The result of the end of historical process gives birth to the notion of liberal democracy. Historical process is the process of dialectical relationship. Subaltern morality brings into limelight the dialectical relationship between elite and subaltern. The new morality contends to transcend this dialectical relationship. Marx advocated class struggle and he aimed to establish classless society. Contradiction is the crux of historical process. Fukuyama observes, "There is not struggle or conflict over 'large' issues, and consequently no need for general or statesmen, what remains is primarily economic activity."[3]

The concept of the end of history is idealistic one. Culture, religion and ethics are put under super-structure and economic phenomena constitute the basic structure. Economic structure or basic structure ignores the idealistic and ethical phenomena. Economic man considers the historical process as materialistic process. Economic man does not attempt to understand ethical thought in its proper perspective. Max Weber in his book entitled "The Protestant Ethic and the Spirit of Capitalism", has contended that the important factors of super-structure are religion, culture and ethics. I think that basic structure and super structures are not cut off from each other. There is integral social structure in which basic structure and super structure are linked and integrated. The divide between two are unwarranted. Subaltern morality believes in inter-relation between basic structure and super structure of society.

The notion of the end of history is not only criticism of Marxism but it depicts the events occurring on the historical scene of the globe. The collapse of communism in Soviet Russia is a great event of history. No one even imagined it before 1989. The question is: what we can conceive in the humdrum of events? We cannot substitute values like sacredness in place of basic necessities like hunger and poverty. Subaltern people suffering from hunger cannot think of idealistic conception of ethics. If we want to progress, we have to delve deep into the basic values of human life. Subaltern morality is the product of social interaction between rich and poor, elite and subaltern. Subaltern people evolve moral values suited to marginalized people. In historical process subaltern moral values emerge. It opts for inclusion and not exclusion. In Indian society hierarchical caste system was based on division of labour but later on it degenerated on rigid caste system. It excludes those who are shudra. Inclusive society does not subscribe to hierarchical caste system. In India there was no conflict and struggle between castes in ancient society. The narrative of class conflict started with the advent of industrialization.

The victory of liberal democracy presupposes the end of communism and rise of nationalism. Nationalism is a great value though we cannot say it as moral value. Every body supports the contention that the rise of liberalism anticipates the end of fascism. Communists do not subscribe to the theory of the end of history and ideology. They still uphold that class struggle and conflicts persist in the society. There is still a struggle between haves and havenots. The dream of Karl Marx to establish classless society has not been achieved through dialectic process. Fukuyama upholds that the greatest victory of liberalism is the rise of classless society. The have-nots are replaced in social dynamics. The emergence of technocrats class have changed the colour of have-nots. The emergence of subaltern morality is the new trend in social process.

Marxism could not achieve its cherished dream of classless society but with the victory of liberal democracy, the value of liberty, equality and justice have emerged. The ideal of classless society to a great extent is questionable. The ethics of old days have given rise to new ethical perspectives. The victory of liberalism is evident in Germany, Japan and America. These nations are supporters of open society and liberal market economy. They encourage globalisation and market economy. This has made a remarkable change in our philosophical perception. After the end of world war an adjustment between idealistic and liberal economy is being perceived in Japan and India.

According to Fukuyama, there is potential danger of nationalism in the wake of liberal democracy. Nationalism is confined to the boundaries of nation. It is not global or universal. Nationalism is opposed to internationalism or globalisation. Amartya Sen in his book entitled "Identity and Violence" observes that nationalism is the potential cause of clashes. Amartya Sen is opposed to nationalism and supporter of globalisation. Amartya Sen asserts that Nationalism is the cause of conflicts. He is against identity and values attached to that identity.

Here I do not subscribe to Amartya Sen's views. To me, it seems quite impossible to transcend Nationalism. To suggest that one should get rid of identity is to suggest that one should skip out of his own body. It is not possible to jump out of his own skin. Nationalism is our identity. We can't get out of national identity as we can't get out of our own skin. Thus I contend that the views of Amartya Sen is not practical. Amartya Sen asserts that Nationalism causes clashes and conflicts and breeds violence. This is not complete truth. Every true nationalist gives importance to the dignity of man and respects the dignity of other Nations. Mahatma Gandhi in his book "Hindswarajya' has emphasized that the feeling of Nationalism is not the potential cause of violent struggle or clash between two Nations. It is our mentality or attitude which causes tension and conflicts. Moreover, it is day dreaming to go beyond Nationalism. One cannot live in abstraction.

In the historical process, struggles have come to an end because classes have been broken. In Indian society the rise of middle class has put a question mark to Marxists division of class as bourgeoisie and proletariat. It has exploded the myth of class struggle because there is no watertight class division as conceived by Karl Marx. Anthony Giddens observes, "Marx's concept of class was always a problematic one, the focus of controversy since at least the time of Max Weber onwards"[4]. Class bound morality has come to end with the emergence of middle class. Post-modernity believes that class struggle is over with the rise of globalisation and liberal democracy. In the history of world-process, the class struggle is no more effective. In post-modern world scene technological problems have taken place. In the rise of post-modernism we go beyond the problem of historical process. The post-historical era is busy with the construction of new social order and new moral values. This new social order will be shaped by technology. The liberals have adopted the world view of technicians. The thesis of endism is used as a means to create a new social order. In post-modern society the technology overshadows ethical standards of life. The philosophy predominantly an Idealistic one in India is undergoing a sort of crisis. Thus, Philosophy has also assumed a techno-critic or instrumental value. The change in tone and temper of philosophy gives birth to 'subaltern morality.'

Fukuyama upholds that the process of the end of history is complete and nothing is left to consider further. We have entered into the post-historical era where technological adjustment in place of speculative ideology is desirable. In view of this development the talk of subaltern morality is relevant. The Indian Philosophy of history is cyclic and the concept of 'Moksha' or liberation is the end of historical process. But in post-modern age, we consider satisfaction of consumer more important than 'Moksha' or liberation. Hence satisfaction becomes a value and 'moksha' has outlived its utility in technological society. Economic calculation is more important than idealism. It is wrong conception that history repeats itself. The history does not repeat itself. I do not subscribe to the view that history repeats itself. In post-modern age, we have the end of history. The question of repetition of history is a myth. In the historical process, a new social order and a new set of values will come up. The emergence of new society will be in accordance with the dreams of technocrat. Liberal policy does not negate the traditional one but it absorbs the essence of tradition and new social structure. Post-modernism anticipates a new social and political order. With the emergence of new social order our ethical standards also have changed. We begin to realise that morality of traditional society will not work. The rise of subaltern creates a new set of value system.

II

After the end of the history the liberal democracy has come up as victorious and new conception of subaltern morality has emerged. I have understood the concept of social development as inclusive development which is integral in nature. By subaltern development. I mean the development in the patterns of life of the marginalised man of the society. It is an attempt to change the life pattern of marginalised people. The change of the life patterns of the marginalised people causes change in the ethical perspectives. In this process, women, dalit, proletariat, marginalised and neglected people attempt to come in the centre stage of social structure. The development means change in the basic structure of society. Basic structure is concerned with economic structure. A critic may raise a question regarding Marxist view of social development because it is mainly concerned with economic factors. Marxist view of development is lop-sided because it does not consider man and society in its entirety. I think that social development is integral process which takes into account both economic as well as cultural phenomena. Abolition of poverty, sustainable development, equality and freedom from exploitation and good governance are incorporated in the notion of development. It is accepted that economic development is important in social development. The paradigm of development has shifted. The change of economic structure is not the sole factor of development. The development incorporates both economic and cultural aspects of human life.

There are many problems creeping in developing nations like India. Some natural calamities like famine, flood, earthquakes obstruct the pace of development. Here I contend that geography plays a role in shaping our values of life. The climatic conditions are linked with life style and value systems. India is a land of poverty amidst plenty. It is essential prerequisite for development that people should be educated and well off socially and politically. Development is considered as change in the economic patterns of life. Modern Indian model of development was primarily concerned with industrialisation and nationalization. But in the post-modern India, there is a significant paradigm shift. Dalit, women and poor people are designated as "subaltern people". They are required to be empowered. In view of the changing standards of development, we have to streamline the role and relevance of philosopher in the context of post-modern conception of subaltern morality.

A philosopher has to recognise the paradigm shift of the notion of development and carry it to illiterate villagers. The question is: who will make subaltern people understand the meaning of capability theory and development as freedom as stipulated by Amartya Sen. Who will carry all these to people? He must be philosopher who can carry all these things to common man and make them understand the paradigm shift of development. A philosopher can point out that sustainable development is ethically desirable and wanton use of natural resources for development is unethical. Who will tell the subaltern people that sustainable development is ethical and rat race for development is unethical? Development is linked with human well-being. Consumerism encourages exploitation of natural resources and ignores the well being of subaltern people who are on margins. Hence consumerism is morally not desirable but development is desirable.

If we do not consider the well-being of the subaltern nations then we are committing a kind of immorality. If we use natural resources in restricted sense and consider the welfare of new generation then we support sustainable development. In sustainable development, we observe the principles of environmental ethics. There is one common point in both capitalist and communists model of development i.e. economic development. Man becomes cog in the wheel of development in both models because capital is an important factor in both models of development. In integral theory of development man is important. This theory contends that human beings are required to be empowered. Man's life can be termed as developed if we consider man as educated, healthy and participating in community life of society. So it is necessary to remove the obstructing factors of development.

Thus, integral development conceives two aspects: one is economic and the other is concerned with ethics. Value aspect is concerned with the quality of life. Development means the development in the quality of life. The process of development brings change in the quality of life patterns. The end point of development is freedom and inclusion of subaltern nation in the mainstream. Man is not only economic and material being. Moral and cultural aspects are also very important in human life. Philosopher alone can streamline these human factors in development.

Philosophers may play a positive role to integral development and improvement of the quality of life of human beings. Economic development is means and not end of development. The consumer culture has distorted the value system of life. It is philosopher's responsibility to maintain sanctity of subaltern morality and sustainable development. Proper distribution of national resources and social justice are also important factors of integral development. By integral development I mean inclusive one. It absorbs the essence of sense, reason and intuition. It includes poor and rich alike. A philosopher has to contemplate about a society free from exploitation and inequality. A philosopher has to underline the paradigms for integral development which is inclusive in nature. The role of philosopher in social reconstruction is important.

The commitment of a philosopher to subaltern morality and national identity is very important. He can't ignore the problem of nation specially the problem of marginalised people to whom I have given the term 'Seemant". The Indian model of development is different from capitalist model or communist model. Gandhi in his Hindswaraj has conceived the Swadeshi model of development. The notion of development can be well understood with reference to geographical and cultural conditions of a nation. Geography affects culture and civilization. Different people of different Nations have different ways of doing and thinking. Everything is affected by the fundamental natural resources and geography of the Nation. The living pattern is determined by geography. It will not be wrong to say that values of life are related to geographical conditions.

The world-views, ideals of life, patterns of existence and moral values are shaped through historical process. Historical process includes geographical conditions. Values of life do not emerge out of vacuum. Cultural values are product of inter-human relationship. A philosopher is also not free from space-time and geography of the Nation. The role of Philosopher is relative to culture and society. The only difference is that Philosopher prepares the path of social reconstruction and subaltern morality. It is a fact that geography has affected the Indian Nation and its cultural and social values. Spirituality is essential features of Indian patterns of life. There is strong relationship between trends of tradition and new tendency of man. We can understand development within the frame works of Indian culture and environment. But new trend of sustainable development is in tune with subaltern morality.

In India we strike a balance between economic affluence and cultural value system. We have developed methods of regulating society and life. We have reconstructed and reformulated the process of development. India is not free from the effects of global market. It is evident that consumer culture has affected our value system. The true development will be both anthropocentric and cosmocentric. Development is concerned not only with the constructions but creation of new set of subaltern value system. A philosopher should attempt to bring those marginalised and subaltern in the centre and redefine the changing paradigms of development. So the development process stipulates dharma or ethical principles. Development without values of man is the development of infrastructure. Development gets meaning when it is linked with human values. It is meaningful if it is inclusive of those who are on margins. This is the reason I call it subaltern conception of development.

References:

1. Giddens, Anthony, A Contemporary Critique of Historical Materialism, Macmillan Press, London, Second edition, P. xi.
2. Fukuyama, Francis, The End of History, 1989, p. 4.
3. Ibid. p. 5.
4. op.cit. p. XV.

CHAPTER – IV

SOCIAL CONFLICTS

In this chapter I acknowledge the book entitled "Identity and Violence" by Amartya Sen which also helped me to understand the notion of religious conflicts and its impact on society and nation. My thoughts have been largely shaped after reading & re-reading few books namely S. Radhakrishnan's 'Religion and Society' and Sri Aurobindo's 'The Human Cycle'. I had been reading 'The End of History and The Last Man' and 'The End of Social Order' by Francis-Fukuyama and 'The Clash of Civilizations' by Samuel P. Huntington. Long back I read the book on "Social Change in Modern India" by M.N. Srinivas who suggested that social stratification is not a closed one but always open. I acknowledge that his concept of 'Sanskritisation' as a significant contribution in the field of social thought. I would like to make a special mention of the book entitled "Manisha Panchkam' by Adi Guru Sankaracarya which is embodiment of subaltern view in the backdrop of Advaitism.

The Manisha Panchakam, a set of five verses by Shankaracharya is the essence of social thought of Shankaracharya. This book helped me to understand the problem of social progress from subaltern perspective. First of all, I got an opportunity to read this text during the lectures in the Chinmay Mission centre of Monoroville, Pittsberg, Pennsylvania U.S.A. When I returned to India I was searching this small text of Sankaracharya. One day in the book stall of Ramkrishna Ashram of Patna. I got the text and read it again and again. I consider it a classical book by Shankaracharya relating to the problem of subaltern morality in the frame work of Advaita Vedanta. I really feel enlightened after reading its content. By social progress I do not mean only economic development or change in the basic structure of society. Social Progress anticipates progress of down-trodden or subaltern. I hold that the true import of Vedanta is to treat human beings equally. The Manisha Panchakam to a great extent helps to mitigate our social problems of discrimination on the basis of caste and prepares the ground for social progress and subaltern morality. The problem of subaltern has been dogging Indian Society for hundreds of years. The Advaita philosophy has never been put into practice otherwise such discrimination and gross exploitation might not have been done. The core of Advaitism is equality of human beings. By 'social progress', I understand that subaltern people who are marginalized need to be progressed and elevated. The social structure is changing very fast. It is generally believed that social stratification is static. Caste is a closed concept. But Prof. M.N. Srinivas has introduced the concept of 'culturalization' which makes the caste not a closed concept but open one. Social stratification is dynamic concept and not static. Subalterns who were marginalized are progressing and occupying the central place in society. By social progress, I do not mean only economic progress but integral progress of human society. Ordinarily, by progress, we mean change in the basic structure of our society and development in economic infrastructure. But this is half truth. By progress, I mean both economic and spiritual progress. By social progress, I understand that underprivileged and marginalized people known as 'subaltern' who have been pushed to the margin since time immemorial should come in the centre stage. By religion, I do not mean only worship to God and observing daily religious rituals. By religion, I mean conservation of values and service to subaltern people. By religion I understand spirituality and service to down-trodden and suffering humanity. Rabindranath Tagore in his book 'Sadhana' says that God resides there where stonebreaker is breaking the stone. I make a distinction between religion and religious fundamentalism. Religious fundamentalism is the cause of social disruption. Sri Aurobindo in his book entitled "The Human Cycle" has made a distinction between religion and religionism. Religionism is negative whereas religion is positive and true guide to human life and society. Sri Aurobindo observes, "There are two aspects of religion, true religion and religionism. True religion is spiritual religion, that which seeks to live in the spirit in what is beyond the intellect, beyond the aesthetic and ethical and practical being of man and to inform and grown these members of our being by higher light and law of the spirit. Religionism on the contrary, entrenches itself in some narrow pietistic exaltation of the lower members or lays exclusive stress on intellectual dogmas, forms and ceremonies, on some fixed and rigid moral code, on some religio-political or religio-social system".[1] The crux of this chapter is social progress in the light of religious ideal so that subaltern or underprivileged may get fair chance and due status in society. Ordinarily, philosophers are charged to analyze religious statements and classify religious statements into cognitive and non-cognitive statements. Philosophers indulge in analyzing religious language. They try to find out logical consistency and scientific certainty. Empty notions and mere fancies for consistency will not work in life. The society is in a critical conditions. We need to concentrate much on religious values and social progress instead of devoting much time in logical chopping and airy philosophizing. Philosophers consider philosophizing as a rational quest and brushed aside religion as anti-progress. Progress does not mean only economic progress. It is progress of total human being. There is great talk about inclusive economic policy. Integral development attempts to reconcile material and spiritual development. The concept of integral is broader one than inclusive development. Inclusion and exclusion are operative at societal level but integral development is at higher level. It integrates national and spiritual levels.

We are at one of the most decisive moments in the post-modern society. People are suffering. They feel anguish of heart. We are living in a post-modern world in which subaltern people have lost their identity. Marginalised men have become shadow of their own images. Radhakrishnan observes, "Ideas inseparable from social decency and justice, which were able to direct and discipline conduct for centuries are swept away. The world is rent by misunderstanding, bitterness and strife".[2] The society is surcharged with uncertainty. The cult of modernism was centrality and rationality but the cult of post-modernism is multiplicity and differences. Modern age was the age of machine. Post-modern age is the age of technology. Technology has created new values and new social order. Traditional religious man clings to old values and does not help to clear the path of new values and new social order. The emergence of subaltern morality is quite new to the present day society. It is new in the sense that it has attempted to relate concepts of subaltern and morality and develop in a philosophical way the concept of subaltern morality.

The social distemper of our life is traceable to the lag between our social institutions and purpose of human existence. Nature has made many races with different religions and social traditions. Man has to create order. Man has to settle differences in order to live peacefully. Radhakrishnan observes that world is not intended to be a battle ground of warring nations, but a common wealths of different groups co-operating in constructive effort to achieve dignity, noble living and prosperity for all. The industrial revolution and technological advancements have affected economic relations between elite and subaltern. Corruption in high places and the inertia of those in power and authority, who wish to preserve the collapsing order and save the crippled civilizations at any cost are loosing their grounds. The social progress is possible either through revolution or reformation of the existing social order. The traditional social structure of Indian society is primarily based on social stratification. The social stratification is based on caste system. The elite of the society is quite well off. But subaltern people who are economically backward and below poverty line are marginalized people. The social progress anticipates the progress of those who are subaltern.

The social progress is through revolutionary change in the existing social conditions. Radhakrishnan observes, "The term 'revolution' need not always imply mob-violence and massacre of ruling classes. Any urgent desire for intense and drastic change of the foundations of civilized life is a revolutionary desire".[3] The term 'Revolution" can be used in two senses (i) a sudden and violent uprising resulting in a coup such as the French or the Bolshevik Revolution; (ii) a gradual transmission spread a period of time from one system of social relations to another as for example, this British Industrial Revolution. What makes a period revolutionary? The fact of change, always present in historical process, but the pace of social change is important in revolution. The present age is revolutionary one because the pace of social change is very rapid. We see that old value systems are breaking. There is change in beliefs and ideals. Sensitive religious people are aware that there is something radically wrong with the present arrangements and institutions in regard to politics, economics and industry. We must get rid of social change if we want social progress and save humanity. A blind impulse to destroy seems to have taken possession of mankind. If there is no check to it, we will take a long stride towards final extinction and prepare for an era of philosophical darkness and ethical barbarism in which man's noblest accomplishments of the past would be laid waste. Radhakrishnan observes, "We live in a period of agonizing strain, of grave anxiety, of manifold disillusionments."[4]

In the post-modern age, we have seen not only material development which is visible but also a definite growth in religious sense and social passion. The representative philosopher of modern age was Karl Marx who denounced religion as opium of the masses. Francis Fukuyama contemplates that in order to get rid of great social disruption, we have to create a 'social capital'. This social capital is storehouse of values. Social values are products of inter-personal relationship and historical process. If we want to escape from great social disruption, we have to go back to our roots. In going back to our roots we have to cultivate religious values which bind society together. It is true that we can't go back to ancient age and turn back the wheel of social progress. It is true that we can't go back to primitive age. The post-modernists explode the myth of Marxism and resort to 'social capital'. They urge to absorb the essence of the past and look towards future. The expression going back to our roots suggests that we have to develop religious identity which binds the entire society together.

If one wants to preserve the social harmony he has to respect 'others'. The question is: can we maintain social harmony in spite of the different religious identities? I think social harmony is must for social progress. Social progress is a process in which social conflict is essential component. Progress is through conflicts. Hegel and Marx contemplated progress through contradictions. Thesis, antithesis and synthesis goes on in the process of progress. But actual progress cannot be an unending process of thesis, anti-thesis and synthesis and synthesis begins to become a new thesis and it continues. After all harmony is required for social progress. Conflicts and contradictions are required to be resolved.

In view of the social conflicts and clash of civilizations the world needs today tolerance and non-violence, and deep concern about the welfare of the poor and the subaltern. Social progress anticipates the liberation of subaltern people from the clutch of poverty. Social progress is possible if and only if there is harmony in society. We are dismayed at the gradual emergence of intolerance, deceit and violence in the individual, society and nation at large. The existence and the gradual strengthening of these dark forces have led to different kinds of conflicts and clashes in society and nations.

Here we deal with the shift of paradigm from economic basis to cultural basis. In the preface of the book "The Clash of Civilizations and the Remaking of World Order". Samuel P. Huntington observed, "Clashes of civilizations are the greatest threat to world peace, and an international order based on civilizations is the surest safeguard against world war".[5] Culture aspires to present a framework, a paradigm, for viewing global politics that will be meaningful to scholars and useful to policy makers. Though in the present time, civilizational paradigm may be helpful but in the end of 21st century it may or may not be meaningful. During the historical process, the paradigm may shift. In civlizational paradigm Huntington emphasizes on religion. As a matter of fact religion is essential component of civilization.

Now, it is in the context of the existence of these dark corners both in the individual and in the society as well. The problem of social conflicts and social progress will be discussed here. Neither the problem of clash nor the desire to find social harmony can ever be treated as new for any age, or epoch in the historical development of man and society. Moreover, the problem of social conflicts and clash of civilizations and its possible solutions are so complex and complicated and so much has been said and written about them by philosophers. Here I propose to examine the nature of the problem of the social progress which anticipates conflicts and a possible solution. Social progress is always through conflicts and contradictions.

The existence of conflict, either in the life of the individual or the society or nation, should not be itself be taken as bad. Conflicts do sometimes lead to progress and prosperity also. But for the presence of such conflicts between what the individual is and what he wants to be, between the life of impulses and desires and that of rationality most of the finest specimen of human species would never have emerged. Socrates, Buddha, Christ, Vivekananda, Gandhi, Muhammad and many other human beings like them would never have been what they were, had they remained satisfied with the situation in which they were born. The conflict and clashes prepared them to be harbinger of social welfare and national dignity. But eternal conflicts and contradictions are not warranted. This is not only true of individuals but of societies and nations as well. No one can deny that human society as a whole has progressed from various sorts of conflicts to a state which can be called a state of civilization. Such a progress has been acquired through stress and strain and by undergoing and overcoming conflicts and clashes. It is why many thinkers have characterized conflict and clashes of civilizations as an indicator of future progress. Stagnant water stinks, so does a society which is devoid of conflicting ripples either from within or from without. Conflicts are the feature of progress. They call for new efforts and new adjustments to taking humanity on a higher step on the ladder of progress, although it cannot be denied that humanity at times has had to pay a heavy price for such progressive adjustments.

But there are conflicts both religious and social which are paralyzing society. Such conflicts, if they are not diagnosed properly and in time, can and do destroy those who suffer from them. The phenomena of psychic repression and regression leading to psycho-pathological sufferings and depressions are the most familiar features of this century. What happens to these mental cases? They fail to adjust themselves to the changing physical and social environment and the result is abnormality and insanity.

India, after her independence, has hardly consolidated herself economically, socially and culturally. The divisive forces of disintegration in the shape of linguism, casteism, regionalism, communalism and in many other ugly forms are creating problems. India has declared herself a secular nation with a number of national languages and has given equality of opportunity and equality before law to all her citizens. Linguistic differences are forces of disintegration. Conflicts on linguistic or religious grounds are no indicator of progress. They are symptoms of a disease which seems to endanger the very existence of our country as a sovereign nation. The life of the nation is run and governed by various institutions-political, economic, cultural, religious and educational-under the supreme and benign care and concern of the sovereign state. These institutions are there to discharge certain functions and attain certain objectives. These institutions are manned by the members of the society who have certain duties and obligations both from the moral and legal points of view. But the root of disintegration has gone so deep into workings of these institutions that they have turned hotbeds of conflicts. The objectives are always lost sight of and the means come to take the place of ends. Howsoever, we may blink and blush, these are the facts which can be gathered from an empirical study of any institutions in India, private or public. It may be a truth, but even the learned associations and societies, institutions of lower or higher education are not immune from this virus. The ruling passions today are not the passions of love and compassion, justice and fairplay, peace and co-operation, but of greed and selfishness, jealousy and rivalry, vanity and love of power. The different political parties in our democracy are not functioning as responsible parties but as sworn enemies of one another, hurling mostly unfounded and unverified charges against one another with the sole purpose of winning elections and grabbing political power. All-pervasive corruption has taken the place of development and welfare. Development is the key word for campaigning but the country remains underdeveloped. The eradication of poverty was great slogan for getting through election but country could not get rid of poverty. Morality of political institutions is at low level. Political morality is at stake in the race of power.

The global picture is no less appalling. It is true that though most of the Western countries have achieved a fair degree of national integration and considerable freedom from internal conflicts which are so much in evidence in Afro-Asian countries. The tragedy of the global situation is that the preparation for the future war started from the day the second world war came to an end. The United Nations Organization was established for the avoidance of future war. The maintenance of 'permanent peace' in the world is desirable. The world has been hot with the cold war. The greatest deterrent to hot war has neither been any wisdom on the part of the warring camps, nor any moral values, but the fear of self-annihilation as a result of the devastating effects of the nuclear weapons. Dr. Radhakrishnan observes, "We are at one of the most decisive moments in the life of mankind. At no other period of human history were so many people bearing such impossible burdens or suffering such agonizing persecution and anguish of heart. We are living in a world in which tragedy is universal. There is a startling relaxing of traditions, of restraints and of established law and order…. The world is charged with suspicion, uncertainty and much fear for the future."[6] This draws a picture of the global scene which continues to be dismal one. Russell had throughout his life, been fighting for the establishment of a sane society. He opted the world free from the destructive passions of hate, rivalry, vanity and love of power and having the positive 'quality of peace'. Russell reveals his mind with regard to the continuing global conflict. "The world in which we live is filled with such collective hatred".[7] The crisis in the life of man is the symptom of the crisis in society. The crisis in society is the symptom of the crisis in human relationship. The disruption in social life creates a great problem for new generation.

India is facing crisis after her independence. The one obvious reason is release of forces which had been suppressed for centuries due to foreign domination. Secondly, that the goods and services to be distributed among the vast population are few and the claimants are more. Such a situation in any social condition is bound to lead inequality and conflict. It is such a social conflict at the base which has converted social castes into political castes, and religious community into a political one. Values and morals are being shattered under the impact of cultural upheavel and new values have not emerged. Thus it leads to social and cultural chaos. The crisis is a transitional one. India has made considerable progress in science and technology. Technology shapes the pattern of human life in twenty first century.

India is struggling to succeed in pulling ourselves out of the conditions of disruption, conflict and social conflicts. India is advanced in nuclear and digital field. The America is very advanced. It is just like a dream world. But dream is at once broken to pieces when we look at the sufferings of the western world or of the developed countries. Erich Fromm in his work, *The Sane Society*, draws a vivid picture of the sufferings of man and society under the monolithic development of economic and political organizations due to application of technology. The technological advancement has just crushed man into nothingness. Technological progress has succeeded in converting man into a cog within wheels. Man seems to have lost his identity. He hardly knows anything of spontaneous joy and happiness. Man has to rush as fast as he can in the race of productivity and efficiency. The cult of consumption has grown. The rat race leads to insanity. The demand for drugs, drinks, and tranquilizers seems to be increasing everyday due to stressful life. Erich Fromm says, "We find then that the countries in Europe which are among the most democratic, peaceful and prosperous ones, and the United States, the most prosperous country in the world, show the most severe symptoms of mental disturbance. The aim of the whole socio-economic development of the Western world is that of the materially comfortable life, relatively equal distribution of wealth, stable democracy and peace.[8] This is the picture of a highly industrialized and technologically advanced society of the west.

Lewis Mumford one of the great intellectuals says that contemporary civilization can produce only mass man, incapable of choice, incapable of spontaneous and self-directed activities. In the present situation man needs moral values for stability of society. In the end, technological society will produce only two groups of men: the conditioners and the conditioned. The rise of middle class in technologically advanced society has changed the structure of society.

What are the implications of such a technological development? In the place of real philosophy we have the philosophy of logical atomism. It is the logical atoms which are considered to be the ultimate constituents of reality. The alienated individuals are taken to be ultimate units of society. The more powerful and finer a machine is, the smaller and subtler are its parts. The cult of individualism is gradually leading to the shrinkage of a man's personality to his inner selfish core. All his relations to other human beings are external to his inner core. The expressions of his love and religious concern, affection and friendship are formal. The technological development has robbed man of his inner core of life. Man is a collection of different kinds of behaviour, physical, linguistic etc. Machine is a collection of its different parts and its behaviour. The individuality of the machine lies in the kind of performance it does. Man is what he performs. Man's utility, value and importance are to be judged in the market of commodities just like other commodities. But for Indian philosophy man is essentially spirit and not robot. Man in essence is not sum total of physical activities. He is a great soul. Advaita Vedanta has contemplated in the oneness of body, mind and spirit.

In the post- modern age man has succeeded in draining out sentiments of love, affection and friendliness. The helpless individual is full of the feelings of animosity, jealousy, rivalry and vanity. He is crushed and repressed under the weight of colossal economic and political pressures. Man is prepared to destroy himself and all others. He takes full revenge for converting him into a cog in the machine.

The situation is paradoxical. Man has prospered but values of life are declining. What are the benefits of the technological knowledge at the disposal of man? The utilization of this knowledge is increasing the comforts of living purely in the physical sense. The physical dimensions of man's pleasures and enjoyments of life have increased beyond imagination. The achievement of technology has given man the most destructive nuclear weapons. Man in general seems to have been cast in the technological mould. Man resembles an idle machine. The machines that man made has succeeded in turning man himself into a machine. Human beings seem to have been reduced to the status of things to be manipulated by big economic and political machineries and manipulators. They have achieved freedom from the basic necessities of life but they are enchained by technology. In this process he has lost his soul. "There is a tragic alliance between the society as a whole and its economic conditions. With a grim relentlessness those conditions tend to bring up the man of today as a being without freedom, without self-collectedness, without independence, in short as a human being so full of deficiencies that he lacks the qualities of humanity."[9]

The dismal picture of the post-modern man and society is obvious. Technology brought into existence such giant social, political and economic organizations as have rendered man helpless. The question is: Is there a way out? Can the freedom of every man to think, to feel and to act as a human being and not as robot be restored? Can man be a fountainhead of soul force, love, affection and co-operation and not that of hatred, rivalry and competition? Can human society grow into that cooperative venture in which there are only friends and brothers and no enemies? The post-modern society is destined to be a society on the lines of the biological evolution where only the so-called fit will survive. If the biological analogy be true of human society, such a society will then be more cruel than animal society. The greed and powers of animals are limited but there is no such limit in the case of human beings.

The more one thinks about the problem, the more he is faced with the same question: Is there any way out? Historically two ways out of such a crisis have been stipulated. First, Philosopher may think that we can bring a revolutionary change. Let man realize that his malice, envy and hatred will consume him along with his fellowmen. Let us realize the efficacy of dharma of moral values in social progress. The champions of this view believe that dharma or moral teachings and practices will bring about a radical change in the personality and society of human beings. The change will bring into existence a peaceful co-operative society. Religious tolerance will bring nations together. Secondly, Philosopher may say that man is the product of religious tradition and social environment. Much cannot be done to change the religious heredity but enough can be done to change the social structure. Man derives social values from his family and educational institutes and institutions. If the social environment is one of malice, envy and jealousy, the individuals, by and large, will imbibe the same spirit. In such a society there may be a few exceptional individuals, who may symbolize man's deeper religious yearning of love and compassion. Individuals are socially and religiously conditioned. If the society is changed man will change. Elucidating the Marxist view in this connection, Radhakrishnan observes, "It is not the consciousness of men that determines their existence, but on the contrary, their social existence determines their consciousness."[10]

Both from the East as well as from the West we have inherited moral, religious and mystic traditions. We have been insisting on the essential unity of mankind. Philosophers of religious studies have called upon people to realize this universal unity. This realization is bound to end all conflicts and disunity, dissensions in the human world. Eckhart, the Catholic mystic of thirteenth century, says, "Then all is one, and one is all. There to her (the perceiving soul) all is one and one is all. Herein lies the soul's purity, that it is purified from a life that is divided and that it enters into a life that is unified."[11] From his point of view "when the soul comes into the light of the super sensual it knows nothing of contrasts".[12] Buddha emphasizes the same vision of unity when he adheres about the ultimate experience of the enlightened in course of his various sayings and teachings. The Geeta and the Upanishads are full of such statements which point towards the vision of such ultimate unity in which all differences and conflicts are negated. In Upanishad the dictum of 'neti-neti' is not negative but points to the ultimate Reality. In Indian philosophy there are certain negative expressions which have positive meanings. Man who realizes this essential unity of values, attains the state of supreme bliss and happiness. All the conflicts and dissensions that are seen in and around man are only on the lower levels. The Advaita Vedanta believes in unity of secular and spiritual values of life. The main attempt of subaltern morality is to put emphasis on inclusive character of social structure. The egalitarian attitude pushes other religions and value system on the margins. They exist only so long as man has not succeeded in breaking through his material cell and transcending into the supreme spiritual self in which all is one and one is all. From the point of view of these saints man is the doer, the actor and the centre of the universe. In Advait Vedanta there is identity of man and Brahman. Shankaracharya perceives that the world full of multiplicities is not real. Multiplicities are expressions of the Brahman. The evils of the world lie in the hearts of men. Man suffers from ignorance. So long as men continue to live on the plane of materiality and in ignorance of their real self, no amount of material progress and social adjustments will make them happy. Though for continued existence bread is necessary, yet men cannot live by bread alone.

If man realizes that 'dharma' according to Hinduism and dhamma in the words of Buddhism are essential to give meaning to life and society then it will be better for humanity. Man and society have been facing crisis through centuries. In the course of the development of human society, there never has been any dearth of good moral precepts and

religious teachings. The ethical values may put an end to
clashes and would usher in an era of all-pervasive peace and
happiness. Erich Fromm rightly points out: "We do not need
new ideals nor new spiritual goals. The great preachers of
the human race have postulated different norms for sane
living. To be sure, they ..... have emphasized different
aspects and have had different views on certain subjects. But
altogether, these differences were small ..... In every centre
of culture ..... the same insights were discovered, the same
ideals were preached. We, today, who have easy access to all
these ideals, who are still the immediate heirs to the great
humanistic teachings, are not in need of new knowledge
of how to live sanely-but in bitter need of taking seriously
what we believe, what we preach and teach"[13] Erich Fromm's
concern is that we do not take seriously human values.
Man has to take human values seriously and implement
them to end the ills and evils of society and nations. This
suggestion appears to be facile and is guilty of the fallacy
of simplification. Fromm seems to be theoretically correct
but practical situation is different. Barring a few exceptional
cases, men have always been drawn more towards the things
of the body than towards the things of spirit. Spiritual and
moral ideals have more often appeared as distant hopes
and wishful dreams in a state of intense individual and
social strife and clash of civilizations. The Socratic principle
of 'Virtue as knowledge', the Christian principle of 'Love
They Neighbours Thyself', the Buddhist principle of
'Compassion' and the Gandhian principle of 'Truth and
Non-violence' appear to be impractical in social practice. In
short, these ideals, though good and desirable in themselves,
have not worked in practice to avoid clashes of civilizations.

Had human beings practiced these ideals the world would not have been what it is today? The world is full of conflicts and clashes. There is always threat of war.

The concept of subaltern morality attempts to make man and his social and global relationship better by making radical changes in the economic and political organizations of globe on the basis of technology. Technology can help us to achieve freedom from economic needs, giving him leisure and money to enjoy life. Actually leisure is essential for philosophizing. There is no doubt that the application of technology to the methods of production led to increase in the wealth of man. It has raised the standard of living of human beings. But what are the fall outs of these. Man is perplexed. He has lost his identity. He has lost his spirit. The thinker, the feeler, and the doer is lost. He is merely a robot in the post-modern technological age. He is the producer and consumer.

The problem is how to give maximum benefits of technology to subaltern people and at the same time save marginalised from being an automaton in the vast economic and political organizations. The problem is how to strengthen the moral values in man and weaken such passions as those of jealousy, rivalry, vanity, love of money and power. Erich Formm suggests the following as a way out of the rut. There is need to rehabilitate man as a free agent, the real doer, thinker, feeler and philosopher, as a real participant in all the economic, political and cultural activities of the society and not as passive agent of a vast machinery. We need relative sharing of wealth and a new and more just division of economic resources amongst subalterns. A cultural renaissance must combine work education for the young, adult education and a new system of popular art and secular ritual throughout the whole nation. Fromm pleads for a simultaneous revolution in the economic, political and cultural spheres for the development of the whole man and whole society. The development of the whole man and whole society is called integral development. Sri Aurobindo in "The Life Divine" stated the integral conception of man's development. He believes that only in such a society man will relate to man lovingly, because all causes for personal, economic and political conflicts will vanish in such a society and in a world community of mutual co-operation and participation. Sri Aurobindo thinks that man gains a sense of self by experiencing himself as the subject of his powers and capacities in the course of social progress.

Human society and social progress have never been stable for centuries. World has seen the defeat and disintegration of seemingly great power like Rusia. It has witnessed the rise of the subaltern people at times. It has seen both the flowering of highest human values as well as mean deeds of man. If we have succeeded in cultivating our intellect to such a great extent, shall we not cultivate our feelings and emotions of love, co-operation, friendship and peace? For this we need a reorientation of our attitudes and values and of the public appraisal of praise and blame in a changed social, national and global context. In the global age of technology conditions for love and co-operation are more favourable than those of rivalry and competition. It appears that a new orientation of our attitudes and values and a re-patterning of our religious, social, economic and political institutions are the pressing need of today. This consciousness on the part of the social philosopher, will elicit adequate response from the vast majority of human beings The new civilization of love, friendship and co-operation, peace and justice is bound to be born. The effort would contribute not only to limiting the clash of civilizations but also to strengthening social progress. The social process are moving into an age when different religions will have to learn to live side by side in peaceful interchange, learning from each other, studying each other's history of religions and ideals and art and culture, mutually enriching each other's religions.

In the end, we can say that the future of social progress depends upon understanding and cooperation among faith leaders of the different religions. In the modern age religion was put to margin, but in post-modern age religion has come to centre stage. Religion is the most important issue for the mankind. Religion has, however, always remained to most important issue ever since the dawn of the human civilizations. Religion has proved to be primary force for social progress, motivating individuals to develop spiritual qualities. It must be acknowledged that the perversion of religion has been a primary cause of social distemper. Social progress is based on moral and religious values. I make a difference between integral social progress and inclusive social progress. Inclusive includes those who are marginalized and integral process harmonies both elites and marginalized. Inclusive has empirical connotation. Integral is spiritual one. The concept of culturalization is quite relevant to understand social progress. Culturalization is a process through which subaltern people will be transformed to higher levels. The process of social progress attempts to purge the social evils of exploitation and marginalisation of subalterns. The concept of subaltern is dynamic one. Social progress anticipates mobility of lower caste to 'higher one'. True religion is neither rituals nor worship of God but it is an attempt to liberate suffering human society.

References:

1. Sri Aurobindo, The Human Cycle, Sri Aurobindo Asharam, Pondicherry, first edition, 1949, P. 215.
2. S. Radhakrishnan; Religion and Society, George Allen & Unwin Ltd; London, 1947, p. 10.
3. Ibid., p. 10.
4. Ibid., P. 11
5. Samuel P. Huntington; The Clash of Civilizations, The Free Press, U.K., 2002, p. 13.
6. S. Radhakrishnan; Religion and Society, Allen & Unwin, London, 1949, p. 10.
7. Russel, Bertand, Human Society in Ethics and Politics, Allen and Unwin, London, 1954, p. 143.
8. Fromm, Erich, The Sane Society, Kegan Paul, 1956, p. 10.
9. Fromm, Erich, op. cit., pp. 223.
10. Radhakrishnan, S. op. cit., p. 57.
11. Quoted in Rudolph Otto, Mysticism: East and West, Macmillan, 1932, 45.
12. Ibid., p. 61
13. Fromm, E. op. cit., 343-44.

CHAPTER – V

SUBALTERN NARRATIVES

Subaltern group of studies in Oxford University has made a significant contribution in the realm of subaltern narratives. But nevertheless it is not totally free from shortcomings. There is no denying the fact that subaltern school has contributed a lot in the study of history, economics and social sciences. Philosophers in the end of 20th century were complacent in doing hair-splitting linguistic analysis.

In the postmodern age analytic Philosophy is outdated. Ordinarily, scholars are prone to consider the question of subalternity with reference to Marxism. Gandhi did not talk in term of subalternity but he has profusely used the expression 'Harijan' which comes under subaltern category. Broadly speaking those who fall beside the circle of power structure are known as subaltern. According to Marxist thought dalits fall within the category of proletariat. They have natural ties with dalits. My contention is that the category of subaltern is different from the category of proletariat of Karl Marx. 'Proletariat' denotes class based on economic structure but subaltern includes caste, class, gender and ethnicity. Marginalized women and blacks are also under subaltern. Hence I consider subaltern as cultural category.

Subaltern morality anticipates two types of moral values. One is elitist narratives who create values and others obey and observe. The another is subaltern narratives which are concerned with the value system created by elites of the society. But I do not equate subaltern with proletariat. This will be wrong to say that subaltern morality is class-bound. Marxist morality is class-bound. Of course, the one view is that the problems of dalit can be fully tackled under the framework of Marxism. The other perspective is that the problem of dalits can be solved in the wake of globalization in natural course of technological development. Gandhi and Ambedkar both are opposed to Marxist view of morality. They do not subscribe to class-bound morality. Gandhi and Ambedkar both decry the notion of globalization. The supporters of globalization may argue that globalization will eradicate poverty and eliminate hierarchical caste system which is a sort of evil of Hindu society. Gandhi and Ambedkar solve the problems of untouchability and subalterniety in the framework of Indian culture and civilization. The question of proximity of Ambedkar with Marxism is out of question. Moreover class concept of Marxism is not comprehensive because it does not take into consideration the gender and ethnicity. Marx considers only economic problems of exclusion but social exclusion is a great problem which still persists in Indian villages. It is true that Gandhi and Ambedkar both distanced from Marsixm. Ambedkar is the representative thinker of dalits who preferred Buddhism instead of Marxism and Christianity. In this respect it will be in the fitness of things that we should refer to a book entitled "Annihilation of Caste" by Dr. B.R. Ambedkar. B.R. Ambedkar observes, "The Speech prepared by me for the Jat-Pat-Todak Mandal of Lahore has had an ashtonishingly warm reception from the Hindu public for whom it was primarily intended"[1]. Ambedkar was supposed to preside over the conference of Jat-Pat Todak Mandal of Lahore. But the conference itself was cancelled because Dr. Ambedkar's address was found by Reception Committee to be unacceptable. The address of Ambedkar might be very explosive. Gandhi observes, "The Committee knew Dr. Ambedkar's views on caste and Hindu scriptures. They knew also that he had in unequivocal terms decided to give up Hinduism."[2]

Gandhi further observes, "It has to be read if only because it is open to serious objections, Dr. Ambedkar is challenge to Hindusim."[3] Ambedkar makes a distinction between caste and varna. There is nothing in the law of Varna to warrant a belief in untouchability. Gandhi observes, "I am aware that my interpretation of Hindusim will be disputed by many besides Dr. Ambedkar that does not affect my position."[4] Gandhi criticises Ambedkar and observes, "In my opinion the profound mistake that Dr. Ambedkar has made in his address is to pick out the texts of doubtful authenticity and value and the state of degraded Hindus who are no fit specimens of the faith they so woefully misrepresent. Judged by the standard applied by Dr. Amebdkar, every known living faith will probably fail."[5] Gandhi in reply to Dr. Ambedkar asserts. "Can a religion that was professed by Chaitanaya, Janayadeva, Tukaram, Tiruvalluvar, Ramrksihna Paramhans, Raja Ram Mohan Roy, Mahrishi Devendranath Tagore, Vivekananda and host of others who might be easily mentioned, so utterly devoid of merit as is made out in Dr. Ambedkar's address."[6]

The philosophical notion of caste and varna is too subtle to be grasped by ordinary people. In the Hindu society caste and varna are one and the same thing for the function of both of them is one and the same i.e. to restrict intercaste marriage and inter-dining. The theory of Varnavyavastha is impossible in this age and there is no hope of its revival in the near future. But Hindus by and large do follow hierarchical caste system and do not want to destroy it. Elites do not feel comfortable to give social equality to the so called untouchables. To seek the help of the shastras for the removal of untouchability and caste is simply to wash mud with mud. It is true that Mahatma Gandhi dissents to the views of Ambedkar. Dr. Amdebkar considers a matter of honour when Mahatma replied to him. It is true that dalits may be vehement critics of caste system of Hindu social structure but they have not totally discarded at any moment. Dalits could not abnegate their caste identity in contemporary India since they have been given constitutional protection and reservations. In ancient India, Dalit or subaltern started movements as "shudra movements". This movement was primarily cultural and social. Marxism divided the society under two classes i.e. bourgeoise and proletariat. The basis of the division was economic. This acknowledges only two classes i.e. 'haves' and 'havenots'. The society progresses through the clash of 'haves' and 'havenots'. Ordinarily dalits fell in the category of have-nots. They fell in the class of proletariat. But when dalit started their movements they discarded the Marxist categories of bourgeosie and proletariate. They became conscious of their own identity as dalits. When dalits became conscious of their identity then they discarded themselves from the category of proletariat.

The main question of dalit discourse or subaltern discourse is whether their problem can be viewed from the economic point of view or cultural point of view. J.S. Mill while doing utilitarianism did not subscribe to Bentham's external standard and hedonistic calculus of hedonism as the parameter of morality. According to J.S. Mill a sense of diginity is the watchword of morality in addition to external measures prescribed conditions by Bentham. It may be said that the question of dignity is deeply related to economic structure of society. In subaltern discourse dalits link their problems to economic hardship and sometimes to dignity of being a human person. Jyotiba Phule emphasized and drew attention towards poverty of dalits. The question of dignity comes afterwards. It is true that proverty is not only social evil but moral evil too. The moral obligation of subaltern lies in getting rid of poverty. Jyotiba Phule was conscious of the fact that education alone can empower dalits. Illiteracy is the one of the major causes of the problem of subaltern. As a matter of fact, the hierarchical caste system has put dalits to the lower or subordinate ranks. They were treated as 'untouchable'. Gandhi defines "untouchability means pollutions by the touch of certain persons by reasons of their birth in a particular state or family. In Hindu society hierarchical caste system is a great source of discrimination. Shudra is put to margin. In the guise of religion, it is always in the way, and corrupts religion"[7]

None can be born untouchable, as all are sparks of one and the same fire. Gandhi very clearly says that, "It is also wrong to entertain false scruples about touching a dead body, which should be an object of pity and respect."[8] But Bhangis, Dusadhs, Chamars and like are contemptuously looked down upon as untouchables caste determined by birth. They are discriminated due to their birth in certain caste. They may bathe for years with any amount of soap, dress well and wear the marks of Vaishnavas, read the Gita every day and follow a learned profession, and yet they remain untouchables. This is 'rank irreligion fits only to be destroyed.'[9] Gandhi is always against untouchability and for upliftment of subaltern whether it may be the case of black in South Africa, dalits in India and negroes in Europe. Subaltern are subordinate and put to margins. We assert our belief that untouchability is not only a part and parcel of Hinduism, but a plague, which is the bounden duty of every Hindu to combat. Every Hindu, therefore, who considers it a sin, should alone for it by fraternizing with untouchables, associating with them in a spirit of love and service, deeming himself purified by such acts, redressing their grievances, helping them patiently to overcome ignorance and other evils due to the slavery of ages, and inspiring other Hindus to do likewise. Further Gandhi holds that removal of untouchability spells the breaking down of barriers between man and man. We are mainly concerned with the untouchability which has received religious sanctions in India. Gandhi appreciated Ambedkar on the score that he was nationalist. He preferred Buddha in place of Marx. Buddha is embodiment of 'dhamma' which comprises moral values and endorses subaltern morality. Ambedkar did not subscribe to Marxist view. Marxist Ideology and class bound morality was not acceptable to Mahatma Gandhi as well as to Ambedkar. Gandhi was influenced by "dhamma' concept of Buddha. Gandhi preferred 'Truth' in place of 'God' because atheists may question the sagacity of God but they will not question 'Truth'. So Gandhi stated that

'Truth is God' and established morality over religion. In Gandhian frame work morality overrides religion. Truth overrides God.

In addition to all these, Ambedkar in his book 'Annihilation of Caste' has incorporated Gandhi's views under Appendix I. A vindication of varna by Mahatma Gandhi on functional basis. In annililation of caste, Ambedkar does not subscribe to Marxism and asserted the identity of dalits. Though it seems a sort of proximity between dalit and proletatiat of Marx. But Ambedkar does not identify 'Dalit' as proletariate since 'dalit' is a cultural category and proletariate is economic category. Dalit could not merge with Marxist concept of class. In ancient India, dalits started movements known as 'shudras movements'. But 'shudras' did not identify themselves with 'proletariate' of Marx.

The question of subaltern narratives is: whether their problems can be viewed from economic point of view, or whether the question of dignity of their existence comes into consideration? As a matter of fact, the sense of dignity is not the external parameters. The question of social exclusion still persists in spite of economic and political empowerment. The question of dignity is linked with the question of social exclusion. Jyotiba Phule drew attention towards poverty of dalits. Jyotiba Phule was conscious of the fact that education alone can empower dalits to stand on their feet. Illiteracy is the one of the major causes of the problems of dalits. As a matter of fact, this hierarchical caste system has put dalits to the lower or subordinate ranks. I consider poverty as a moral evil. The moral obligation of society lies in getting rid of poverty. As a matter of fact, the hierarchical caste system has put dalits or subalterns to the lower or subordinate rank. They were treated as 'untouchables. In civilized society 'untouchability' is a curse. So we should free society from 'untouchability. The crux of the subaltern narratives lies in empowering those who are on the margins of power structure. It becomes moral obligation and bounden duty of civilized citizens to undo the practice of untouchability prevailing in Indian society. Gandhi was dead against untouchability. He considered 'untouchability' as a moral evil. In order to get rid of this social evil of untouchability, Gandhi changed the nomenclature of "shudras" as 'Harijans'.

The problem of 'untouchability' was taken by Gandhi and he termed shudra's as 'Harijans' in order to change the perception of general mass. Gandhi aspired to free and raise the status of 'shudras'. He wanted to remove the prevalent practice of 'untouchability'. In 1972, few young dalits formed a group known as 'Dalit panthers' in Maharastra in order to liberate the 'shudras' from the oppression. Dalit panthers fought the battle to restore the dignity of dalits. But in short period the 'Dalit Panthhers Group' dwindled. Dalit Panthers faced a division. The two views emerged within 'Dalit Panthers'. Some of the members adhered to Ambedkarvada and few others lapsed into leftism. The ideologicisal conflicts created divison among them. There were some thinkers who adhered leftism alongwith Ambedkarvada. In 1960, the narratives of dalit problem started afresh in cowbelt and leftism reappeared. Dalit associated themselves with the category of proletariat. But dalit narrative is different from the narratives of proletariat. Dalit problem is not only economic but social also. Dalits face economic inequality as well as social exclusion. They are being exploited due to economic backwardness and hierarchical caste system. Some of the thinkers tried to reconcile Ambedkar with Marxism. Some of the thinkers tried to find similarities and differences between Gandhi and Ambedkar. Economic backwardness of dalit is directly linked with hierarchical caste system of Indian society. They think that Marxism must be combined with Ambedkarvada in order to get rid of dalit problems. Leftist were dreaming that class system will replace the caste system of Indian society. Sublatern morality holds that we have to deconstruct the age-old value system conceived by Brahminism or Marxism. By Brahminism, I do not mean any caste as Brahmin but it stands for elitism in Indian society prevailing through out the history. On the one hand, subaltern morality deconstructs age old traditional values of Hinduism and on the other hand it makes departures from Marxists views on moral values. Subaltern morality is different from Marxist morality. Subaltern morality in post-modern society gives emphasis on feminism and its importance to liberate women from supression.

But dalit thinkers could not subscribe to Marxism. Philosophers did not agree to reconcile Amebdkarvada with Marxism. Indian Marxist dreamt to establish communism in India without disturbing the hierarchical caste system. As a matter of fact, Marxism failed to ameliorate pathetic conditions of downtrodden. In the meantime, Marxism collapsed. Marx was considered the representative thinker of modernism. Modernism lapsed and post-modernism emerged as the cult of 21st century.

Dalits kept patience for long years but now they are restless to deconstruct the centre of power and trying to enter into the mainstream of power structure. The power decides the role of a person in the present day political and social structure. Dalit women have not been included in the framework of Marxism. They have to search a way out. The promise and movements of Marxists could not solve the problems of dalit women. Dalit women assumed aggressive postures in the present day in Indian society. Marxism was in defensive box relating to 'dalit vimarsha'. Some of the thinkers of Marxist brand may say that Marxism includes gender problems. But this is far from truth. Feminism is against gender inequality. Karl Marx could not address the aspect of inequality based on gender discrimination and confined their discourse on economic basis. In Hindi belt, the exploitation of dalit women is a common feature. In the beginning, Bihar did not witness any dalit movement. Earlier philosophers did not take the social problems and its applied aspects. They were self contended with metaphysical subtleties and hair-spliting analysis. The non-dalits have tried to work out the sketch of sufferings and exploitations of dalit in the similar veins as dalit thinkers have done. 'Dalit Vimarsha' should not be closed within forewalls of dalits alone but should be opened. It should not be confined to caste structure. Subaltern narratives should not encourage closed attitude towards the problems. Indian philosophers have taken a sympathetic view towards dalit problems. Gandhi dwelt on the problems of subaltern in his own way. He realized the panges of sufferings and exploitations and tried to liberate 'shudras' and called them Harijans. We have to take into account Gandhian perspective towards subaltern. Gandhian view is to improve the social condition of subaltern and give them due importance. Gandhi was having an open attitude and tried to fight the problem of untouchability alongwith dalits. Dalit movements could not align with Marx rather they followed Gandhi. Gandhian perspective did not perceive that society will be class-less. Marxist are outdated since they did not imagine the emergence of middle class in their class-structure. Marxist were stuck to 'Das Capital'. It seems that they are unaware of the rapid growth of middle class. They are quite in dark that class-division has taken a different shape in the wake of globalization. In fact, they did not properly understand the problem in its entirety. They did not conceive that the end of bourgeoisie or capitalism or class-division is not the end of sufferings of subaltern people of India. They will have to face the problem of hierarchical caste system and its social exclusion. Dalits have to fight against the exploitation on the basis of caste system within the Indian framework of social structure. Marxist failed to understand the problems of Indian Subalterns. Ambedkar considered that without annihilation of caste, we can't establish classless society as conceived by Karl Marx. It is sheer bookish to contend that we can achieve class-less and exploitation free society. The caste system in India is first and then the question of class comes. Marxist philosophy was rejected by Baba Saheb Ambedkar. The caste system is not only based on the division of labour according to Bhim Rao Ambedkar rather it is division of labourers. Baba Saheb in his famous book 'Annihilation of Caste' conceived that any reform on the basis of economics in Indian context will be secondary and imcomplete. But in social development, we have to take into consideration both economic and social factors. Development is inclusive process. Baba Saheb thinks that caste system is a problem. Gandhi also contemplated that the prevailing social problem is primarily linked with both economics and social structure. Any reform or revolution can't be effective unless it struggles with the prevailing social discrimination and exploitations. Gandhi paid due attention to problems of subaltern and down-trodden. Unless we solve the caste problem, we can't proceed towards establishment of society free from inequality and exploitation. In Indian context Gandhian perspective alone is relevant to solve the social problems of Indian life. Marxism does not understand the problem of caste subalternity. In Indian context, we can say that Marxist philosophy is not applicable since caste based structure was inconceivable to Marx. Dalit discourse can achieve its goal not in the Marxist framework of philosophy but in Gandhian philosophy of village reconstruction and development. Dalit problem in India is great problem of villages. In cities, we have liberated from caste to a great extend due to economic upliftment, social mobility and development in education. Unless we tackle the problem of untouchability, we can not contemplate about the total reform. Buddha does not subscribe to caste system. He deconstructed vedic social structure based on varna which degenerated into caste structure.

When we observe the poverty in the subaltern locality of villages, we are simply shocked. People suffer from great hunger. Sometimes it seems that the main problem of subaltern is economic. The poverty prompts us to come to the view that the main problem of subaltern is social exclusion. Mahatma Gandhi realized that it is not only economic but social and cultural. He advocated education as a means to improve the conditions of subaltern. Education is great liberating force and can reform the pitiable conditions of subaltern. I contend that solution to dalit problem is neither in Marxism nor in Ambedkar's philosophy of caste annilitation. It is in Gandhian philosophy of removal of untouchability and reconstruction of village economy. Here Amebdkar conceived and gave the call to dalits to migrate to cities and get rid of problems. But Gandhi contemplates reconstruction of villages and end the system of 'untouchability'. Jyotiba Phule as well as Amebdkar consider the dalit problems as social and not only economical. Suhdras are deprived of education since the time immemorial. Subaltern were deprived of fundamental rights from early stages of civilizations. As a matter of fact, Amebdakar talks about economic problems but is not a Marxist. Ambedkar realized that Dalits have to fight against identity crisis. The identity discourse is unique in itself. It can't be mixed up with other problems. Even if economic problem is dominant in subaltern discourse, we can't identify economic identity with that of caste identity of Indian society.

Subaltern narrative streamlines the discrimination done to them in the historical process of social development. The identity of schedule caste and schedule tribe is not only linked with poverty but they are marginalized even if they are economically well off. They are under the category of subaltern that stands for marginalized people. Subaltern narrative cannot be confined to economic discourse. Subaltern narrative puts their problem in full blooded way. The schedule caste and schedule tribe are suffering from the problem of social exclusion. They have been put on reservation not only due to economic backwardness but due to social exclusion. There is significant distinction between the concept of poor and proletariate. Proletariat is the bye product of industrialization which emerged during the 19th century in England. Subaltern are poor and marginalized but they can not be equated with proletariate. Subaltern is inclusive of working class but it is not limited to proletariate.

This is obvious that Marxism and Gandhism have different perspectives towards the problem of subaltern. The economic problem of subaltern can't be ignored in the social problem of Indian society. The demand of subaltern is related to their identity and dignity. In cowbelt the Marxist movement and dalits movement are quite different. If dalits are on the margins not only on the grounds of economics but they are being dubbed as 'untouchables'.

Now I will come to the philosophical implication of globalization and subaltern movement. The cult of marketism in postmodern age will certainly affect the problem of subaltern movement. The one perspective is that dalits will have comfortable position in the age of globalization. They will get opportunity to earn money and live a decent life. The other perspective is that subalterns will be thoroughly marginalized in the post-modern age. The one perspective holds that globalization is favourable for subalterns and the other perspective is that it is against the prospect of subaltern. The globalization will put subaltern on the margins since money is the measure of everything. A philosopher may conceive that caste does not affect global market. Globalization does not influence caste system. Globalization will help to develop skills of each caste with the victory of liberal democracy and emergence of globalization. Skill will improve the condition of subaltern.

It is true that capitalism is committed to profit making business. The capitalism has its own philosophy of profit. Those dalit thinkers approve globalization as panacea for inequality and caste discrimination are possibly not correct. Foreign investors are not interested in social problems of the nation. After the collapse of communism, liberal democracy has come victorious. But globalization transcends the concept of national Identity as well as caste identity. I contend that national identity is an important factor. Globalization blurs national identity. The character of capitalism affects the national identity. I think subalterns will be most affected in the wake of marketism. Those who are on the margins will be pushed further on the marginal point. The welfare work of nation will be affected by globalization. The swadeshi culture propounded by Gandhi will be best course for subaltern people of India.

References:

1. B.A Ambedkar, Annililation of Caste, 1937, Preface of the second edition. Appendix A Vindication of Caste by Mahatma Gandhi (A Reprint of his Article in the Harijan July, 16, 1936)
2. Ibid., p. 1
3. Ibid., p. 2
4. Ibid., p. 6
5. Ibid., p. 6.
6. Ibid., p. 6.
7. Shriman Narayan (editor) "The Selected Works of Mahatma Gandhi", Navjivan Publishing House, Ahmedabad, 1968,p.235.
8. Ibid.
9. Ibid.

□□□

CHAPTER – VI

SUBALTERN MORALITY
IN POST-RAMAYANA RAMKATHA

This chapter is an attempt to analyse the concept of subaltern morality in the context of post-Ramayana discourse. This attempts to streamline subaltern ethical problems spread in some versions of post-Ramayana Ramkatha. The first author of Ramayana is Valmiki. He has composed it in Sanskrit which is the language of scholars and elitist of the society. Ramayana is the national manual of ethics. Moral life is the primary object of human existence. Ramkatha is a great guide to our moral behaviour. The Encyclopaedia of Religion and Ethics contends. "Probably no work of literature, secular in its origin, has ever produced so profound an influence on the life and thought of a people as the Ramayana".[1]

It is quite difficult to go through the entire Ramkatha literature written in different languages. The Ramayana is very aptly characterised by Hopkins as a "Concordant Discord" or more appropriately a concordant full of discord. The original Ramayana by Valmiki was a harmonious whole and that the dicordant elements in it were due to accretions which had taken place over a long period. The Ramayana is not history or biography. It portrays the human drama and moral conflicts.

In Valmiki Ramayana, Rama is depicted as a great and unique person not as an incarnation of God. I have understood Rama as a purusotam Rama who suffers ups and downs of life and upholds the moral values. In order to understand the problem of 'subaltern morality' spread in Post-Ramayana Ramkatha literature, I will prefer to concentrate on Kamba Ramayana, Kritivasa Ramayana and Tulsi's Ramcharitmanas.

The expression 'subaltern' is the post-modern one. By 'subaltern morality', I mean a sort of morality which gives a rightful and honourable position to those who have been marginalised since long. I have tried to give the Post-modern treatment to Post-Ramayana Ramkatha. I am very clear that Post-Ramayana is not post-modern, but there is no harm in giving a new treatment. I have taken up the problems of morality relating to underpriviledged in epic period. I have tried to rethink the problems of morality in the light of Post-Ramayana Ramkatha and give a post-modern treatment. I uphold that 'subaltern morality' deconstructs the age old traditional conception of morality. It deconstructs the totalitarian concept of morality. The post-modern morality is relative. In the Post-modern age, we conceive a change in the moral value system. It is generally believed that egalitarian morality has been the corner stone of Indian social structure. In epic period, Brahmanism was in the centre and subalterns were on margin. By subalterns, I mean under priviledged. I contend that if we meticulously examine the Post-Ramayana Ramakatha literature, we find that 'others' were given due position. Post-modernism contemplates that those who have been marginalised earlier have staged a comeback in the centre. Sri Ramacharitamanas of Tulsidas is the most authentic book of Post-Ramayana Ramakatha literature. This has equally appealed to the lowly and affluent. By 'subaltern morality', I contemplate that those who are untouchables and downtrodden should be given rightful place. It is immoral to treat them as untouchable. My central aim is to emphasise that in Post-Ramayana Ramakatha schedule caste and schedule tribe have been given rightful place except few exceptions. The post-modern approach is a new way of seeing the world. It resists the grand narratives and subscribes to multinarratives. Here Jean Francois Lyotard's contribution is important. Christopher Butler observes, "Lyotard argued in his 'La Condition Post-moderne' that we now live in an era in which legitimizing 'master narratives' are in crisis and in decline"[2]

By master narratives in the context of Ramacharitamanas, I understand Purohitvadi mindset of Indian society. Purohitvadi narratives are contained in or implied by Ramacharitamanas. Here I am attacking on the grand narratives of purohitvada. If the same soul pervades in each individual and the same blood flows in each man, why somebody should be deprived on the basis of caste and somebody should be priviledged. I am suggesting that in Post-Ramayana Ramkatha schedule caste and schedule tribe have not been marginalised as it is usually believed. I consider that master's morality has lost its credibility in post-modern era. The basic attitude of post-modernist was a scepticism about the claims of any kind of overall, totalizing explanation. Lyotard was not alone in seeing the intellectual task of 'resistance' even to 'consensus', which 'has become an outdated and suspect value. Christopher Butler contends "Postmodernists responded to this view, partly for the good reason that by doing so they could side with those who didn't 'fit' into the larger stories - the subordinated and the marginalised - against those with the power to disseminate the master narrative."[3] I understand that Post-Ramayan Ramakatha does not harbour unethical attitude towards S'hudra as a class. I have dealt the problem of S'hambukvadha and tried to streamline its ethical implications. I have understood Hindu ethics in two ways. One is philosophical, another is popular. Philosophical hindu ethics is based on Vedas and Upanisad: whereas popular Hindu ethics is based on Mahabharat and Ramayana. I have tried to discuss moral conflict in epics. I have mainly dealt with the problem of sub-altern morality concerning Shambukvadha. I have not used the expression 'dilemma' in strict technical sense. I have used it in common paralance. The dilemma arises when we are perplexed to decide as what to do and what not to do. It becomes difficult to determine which action is morally justified or unjustified. A dilemmatic situation arises in Uttar-Rámáyana relating to Shambukvadha. Ráma is in a fix to determine whether killing of S'hambuk is morally justified or not.

In dilemma there are two alternatives. If we accept one and negate another, then the matter is complicated. Two alternatives are known as horns of dilemma. As we know that if we are in between two horns of buffalo, we can not escape from being hurt. In case of Shambuk, Rama is also between two alternatives. If he kills Shambuk then he is liable to be accused of being prejudicial and anti-shudra: if he does not kill, he is not performing the duty of a king because he is not protecting the subjects. At last, he has to break the horns of dilemma and he preferred to perform the duty of king and protect his subjects. In this sense, I have taken up the case of Sambukvadha as moral dilemma.

The treatment of shudra in the Ramcaritamanas raises some ethical questions. In ancient time the attitude of Hindu scriptures and society were not quite favourable towards Shudras. Here we want to dwell on sub-altern morality of Hindu society in the context of Post-Ramayana Ramakatha literature. The expression subaltern morality in Post-Ramayan Ramakatha requires explanation. The word subaltern stands for the meaning as given in the concise Oxford dictionary, that is 'of inferior rank'. It will be used as a term for the general attitude of subordination whether this is expressed in terms of class, caste, age, gender and office. The Subaltern Indian Philosophy attempts to rewrite Philosophy and write about society from a people's viewpoint and not from elite point of view. I have tried to concentrate on the Varna dimension of subalternity in Post-Ramayan Ramakatha. The subordination and subjection that marks the life of Nishad and Shabri in Post-Ramayan Ramakatha bring them into the centers. By subaltern morality, I mean morality of marginalised people. Untouchables (Dalit) have retained their identity as a subordinated people during epic age. Dalit in the epic period share in the state of subalternity. Subaltern morality is concerned with the justice to subordinate Nishad and Shabri of Rāmakatha. Rāma brought the dalit in the centre. The marginalised dalits were brought to centre. The marganalised Shudra can be termed as the 'Other'. Rama gave rightful place to 'the Other'.

B.R. Ambedkar in his book titled "The Riddle of Hinduism" upholds that the Ramacaritamanas is against Shudra. As regards the summary execution of the ascetic S'ambuka the alleged action of Rama has been criticized by him. Rāma killed Shambuk, a shudra doing penance in order to attain godhood, when no shudra was allowed to do penance. Rama considered his pious duty as a king to punish Shambuk for what he thought to be a sin or adharma. A brahmin arrives at his palace gate carrying the dead body of his son, and laments, blaming the king for the death of the child.[4] The brahmin said that there must have been some evil deeds performed by Rama due to which immature death of some children occurred in his territory. The subjects who are not protected rightfully perish on account of the faults of kings, when a king is not rightful, his people die untimely death. "Narada told Sri Rama the causes of the death of Brahmin's son as an unauthorized practice of penance by a Shudra".[5] This episode of Shambukvadha has been added by Valmiki in Uttar-Kanda to project the image of Rama as a king who did not hesitate to uphold the varna system prevailing in the age. Rama found S'ambuka practising penance and violating the asigned varna dharma. He executed the culprit and the dead brahmin boy became alive. Kamban omits this part of Uttarkanda. In Ramayana the event of Shambukvadha occurred earlier than Aswamedha Yajna. Bhavabhuti in his Uttarramcharitam has changed the sequence of the events narrated in the Ramayana. He has linked the event of Shambukvadha with Aswamedha Yajna. In Ramayana due to the death of Shambuka, the people started condemning Rama the king. In view of public stricture, he consulted the important gurus like Vashistha and others and called a meeting of all important risis. In that meeting Narada discloses the premature death of a Brahmin boy is due to penance of Shudra Shambuka. Rama was asked to follow his Rajdharma. Here we find that the theme of Uttarramcharitam of Bhavbhuti is different in substance from the Uttarkanda of Valmiki Ramayana. Rama faces a moral dilemma because he is king of Ayodhya. He gives preference to Rajdharma. Bhavabhuti infuses Rajdharma in Rama. The only way to make alive the Brahminputra is to kill the Shudra Shambuka. In order to maintain the grace of Rajdharma and save the life of Brahminputra, the only course open to him is to kill Shambuka. Rama, on the one hand, is moved by Rajdharma and on the other hand, moved by pity towards Shambuk. In the end, Rajdharma prevails. He controls the feeling of pity towards Shambuka and accomplished his Rajdharma.

It transpires from the above episode that Purosotam Rama also favoured a Brahmin and killed a Shudra for observing penance. The standard of morality in that age was the prevailing varnadharma. Now the question arises: whether the killing of Shambuka is morally justified or not? Valmiki Ramayana could not justify this event. Tulsi simply omits this incidence in the Ramc'aritmanas like Kamban. But it is not justified, according to some followers of Tulsi, to say that Rama looked down upon the Shudras as a class. Nisad, Kevat and Shabri are living witnesses to this contention. If Tulsi harboured any unethical attitude towards sudras as a class, then he could not have endowed these characters with the nobility. Manthara, the hunch-backed maidservant, was instrumental in causing Bharat to be given the throne and Rama being exiled. She is described as of a low caste. Does this observation mean that a low caste person is looked down upon with contempt? This could hardly be so. Manthara was crooked but Tulsi does not castigate aspersion against the humble class as a whole.

When Bharat goes to meet Rama in the forest, Nishad was apprehensive at the sight of his huge army. But Nisad was mistaken. Taking Nisad to be a devotee of Rama, Bharat embraces him. After seeing this scene, gods rain flowers on him. His body thrills to meet one who is considered Sudra in society. We can hardly blame Tulsi for harbouring ill will and an adverse ethical attitude towards sudras. When Rama, Laksmana and Sita leave Ayodhya, they reach the village of Nisadraj. Nisad warmly welcomed them. Rama pays great attention to Nisad and asks him to sit near him.[6] Nisad serves Rama, Laksmana and Sita, fruits of the forest with his own hands. He gives him water to drink. It is clear that Rama makes no distinction between a Sudra and a Brahman. He treats them alike "When he perceived his unfeigned affection, Rama took him with him and Guha was overjoyed".[7] Tulsi calls Nisada Rama's sakham. Nisad too considers that there is no honour so great as to die thus in Rama's service. When Bharat and the army and citizens of Ayodhya are staying in the forest, the Kols, Kirats and Bhils, all people of schedule caste and tribes, offer them delicious fruits of the forest. I consider Kols, Kirats, Bhils as subaltern people. As a matter of fact schedule tribes are subaltern. The citizens offer to pay them handsomely but they refuse to take money. In a voice full of love they said; "Do not slight our love by paying us, or returning what we offer. You are noble and we are humble sudras".[8] These words have been said by the Bhils of the forest in a spirit of humility. In fact, Nisad feels the nobleness of the treatment meted out by Rama and Bharat. He says, "I am a man of low caste and the doer of degrading jobs. Even then the external lords of the universe, Bhagwan Rama has shown his grace to such a fallen creature as me."[9] This episode has clearly established that Rama gives important place to marginalised schedule caste and tribe. This amply shows that in Post-RamayanRamkatha subaltern are given due importance.

Here a student of Valmiki Ramayana will see how much more delicate is Kamban's Guha, when compared to Valmiki's Guha. V.V.S. Aiyer observes. "It would be worthwhile to compare the whole episode of Guha as treated by Kamban at every step with Valmiki's treatment of the same. Valmiki has worked wonders in this episode but even the most partial admirer of Valmiki will have to admit that the touches that Kamban has added to it make it more entrancing, more grand".[10]

When Rama wandering in the forest in search of Sita, he happens to slay a demon of the name of Kabandha. The demon under a curse for having insulted the sage Durvasa. It so happened that Kabandh who is a gandharva, was singing in Indra's court. He found Durvasa Rishi indifferent and inattentive to his song. He said harsh words to the sage about it. Durvasa Rishi cursed Kabandh to become a demon. While killing the demon Kabandh, Rama says, "Listen, O Gandharva, I do not like one who bears malice towards Brahmins, Brahma, Siva, and the other gods and I too are at the bidding of one who serves Brahmins. A Brahmin is to be worshipped even if he speaks harsh words, imposes a curse, or chastises - so the sages say. Even if a Brahmin is devoid of gentleness and virtue he is to be worshipped, and a sudra, even though replete with all good qualities and deeply learned, is not to be worshipped".[11] Can we say that these words of Rama to Kabandha are derogatory of Sudaras? On the face of it, they may seem so. But this is the expression of the prevailing conditions of the society of that age to which Tulsi belonged. According to Shastras, a Brahmin was to be revered, when Tulsi makes Rama say all that mentioned above he also adds, so the sages say.[12]

When Rama and Laksmana go to Sabri, a Sudra woman, she embraces their feet and is overwhelmed with joy. Rama and Laksmana accept the fruits of the forest which Sabri tastes firsts and sets before them to eat. Rama says to her, "I only recognize the bond of devotion, nothing else".[13] To Sabri, Rama gives the high place of honour which is difficult even for saints to get. He says, "In you all the various kinds of devotion are deeply entrenched. Therefore, the state which is difficult for sages to attain you have reached today without any effort."[14] It is clear from the above quotation that Rama's stress is not on caste superiority but on bhakti. It transpires that Shudras like Kevat, Shabri and Nishad, who are full of devotion are considered by him more distinguished than others. Rama says, "I recognize no relationship except that of faith".[15] Thus, Tulsi disagreed with the exclusivistic views of the 'extreme' position of orthodox Hindus. The old traditions and tales get a new and up-to-date interpretation at the hands of the epic master. This ability to retain the old while accepting the new is an important feature of Hindu life. Tulsi's Ramarajaya stands for social justice, for kindness to the entire population, whether high or low.

REFERENCES:

1. Hastings, James (ed.); Encyclopaedia of Religion and Ethics, Vol. X (T.T. Clark, Edinburg, Third edition, 1952), p. 574.

2. Christopher Butler; Postmodernism, Oxford University Press (Second Impression of Indian edition), 2007, p. 13.

3. op.cit., p. 15.

4. The Ramayana (Canto LXXII, Sanskrit Text with English Translation, Pt III, Uttara-Kanda, Gita Press, Gorakhpur, Third edition 1992), p. 2126.

5. Ibid, Canto LXXIV, p. 2127.

6. Pumchhi Kusal Nikat Baithai.
   The Ramcharitamanas, Ayodhyakanda, 87: 2.

7. Sahaj Saneh Rama lakhi Tasu linha Guha hridaya hulasu
   The Ramcharitamanas, Ayodhyakanda, 103-4.

8. The Ramcharitamanas, Ayodhyakanda, 249-3.

9. Ibid; 195.

10. Aiyar, V.V.S.; Kamba Ramayana: A Study; (Bhartiya Vidya Bhavan, Bombay, 1987, p. 273.

11. The Ramcharitamanas, Aranyakanda, 32: 4 & 33:1.

12. Ibid; 33: 4., Gavahim Santa.

13. Ibid., 34: 2.

14. Ibid., 35: 4.

15. Kah Raghupati Sunu Bhamini bata manaum ek bhagati karnata.
    Ibid., 34: 2.

CHAPTER – VII

GLOBAL JUSTICE

I contend that the concept of global justice is based on the theory of distributive justice as stipulated and contemplated by Aristotle. To deal with the ethical legacy of Socrates, Plato and Aristotle is vast and quite extensive. I have concentrated myself on Aristotelian conception of distribute Justice in global society. I propose subaltern conception of global justice which is based on Aristotelian conception of distributive justice. Socrates, Plato & Aristotle attempt to change the existing social order of pre-socratic society. Aristole's theory of justice is distributive in nature. In Aristole's view, justice is concerned with the regulation of human relations. Distributive justice deals with the allocation of honours and wealth. Its basic principle is "treating equals equally and unequals unequally". Aristotle preferred to rely on the prevailing customs and customary laws for deciding as to who were equals or unequals.

I think globalization as process of development is just and globalization as an instrument of exploitation is unjust. Globalization is faced with a paradox. If we go against globalization, then we will be technologically backward and condemned to be poor and underdeveloped. The backwardness will cause poverty. As a matter of fact, poverty is a moral evil and responsible for many immoral activities. So in order to get rid of poverty and backwardness we have to accept technology based globalization. Peter Singer observes, "One hundred and fifty years ago, Karl Marx gave a one-sentence summary of his theory of history: "The hand mill gives you society with the feudal lord; the steam mill, society with the industrial capitalist. Today he could have added: the jet plane, the telephone, and the internet give you a global society with the transnational corporation and the World Economic Forum".[1] Technology has changed everything. But the development of technology and globalization causes dehumanization. Technology is very much advanced. Life is deeply conditioned by technology. Man is alienated from himself. Man becomes a cog within the wheel. Dehumanization is equally evil. So we are faced with paradox of globalization. Globalization is linked with development. Development is linked with well being of humanity. Sustainable development is morally desirable. Wanton development is morally undesirable.

Secondly, I contend that global justice is not logically incompatible with national identity. This idea has been shaped by studying the three notable books relating to the problem of global justice and national identity. The book entitled "The World is Flat" by Thomas Friedman who gives a brief history of twenty first century scenario of global development. This book gives a vivid account of globalization. It makes us to see this globe in a new perspective. We have no idea as to how the 21st century history will unfold in the age of globalization. Friedman explains how the flattening of the world happened at the dawn of the 21st century. The world is flat means that the world has become a global village. The world has become too small. The world has become a global village due to fast pace of communication. Friedman says after his return from the Bangalore city of India, "Columbus reported to his king and queen that the world was round, and he went down the history as the man who first made the discovery, I returned home and shared my discovery only with my wife and only in whisper. "Honey confided, I think the world is flat"[2]. The another book entitled, "The Clash of Civilization and the Remaking of World Order" by Samuel Huntington also helped me to understand the problem of Globalization and National Identity. Henery Kissinger commented that this is one of the first chapter of this book reads "Flags and Cultural Identity". In the very opening sentence of the introduction the problem of identity has been discussed. Huntington says that global politics has become multicivilizational. In the late 1980s the communist world collapsed. The cold war became history. The most important distinction among nations is not ideological, political, or economic but cultural according to Huntington. In the words of Samuel Huntington "Nation states remain the principal actors in world affairs.[3] After reading these books I tried to work out that these two problems are not logically incompatible as it appears. Peter Singer wondered that the most influential work on the conception of Justice is John Rawls's "A Theory of Justice". In this book John Rawls failed to discuss the issue of global injustice. Peter singer observes "I was astonished that a book with the title, nearly 600 pages long could utterly fail to discuss the injustice of the extremes of wealth and poverty that exist between different societies".[4] I think that John Rawls conceptions of justice as a fairness presumed that this world is not just. This is true that we do not live in the just and fair world, John Rawls observes, "I will comment on the conception of justice presented in "A Theory of Justice" a conception I call" justice as fairness".[5] The question is: what is global Justice? It is not very clear as to what global justice means? In this connection I mention the book titled "The Idea of Justice" by Amartya Sen. Prof. Sen begins with the conception of injustice in order to understand justice because he understands justice as the absence of injustice. He focuses on comparative judgements of what is "less" of more "just". At the heart of Sen's argument is a respect for reasoned differences in our understanding of what a just society really is. Amartya Sen upholds that identity causes violence. National identity is a fact and not figment of imagination. Tolstoy in his most celebrated book "War and Peace" upholds that national identity is the root cause of war. Amartya Sen in his book titled "Identity and Violence" adheres that national identity is the cause of violence. Hence Tolstoy as well as Amartya Sen in order to avoid war and violence suggested to transcend national identity. They advocated universalism and globalization. They discarded national identity. But I do not subscribe to the views of Tolstoy and Amartya Sen. To suggest that one should transcend national identity is to suggest that one should skip out of his own skin. So the suggestion of Tolstoy and Amartya Sen is not practical.

Thirdly, my contention is that global justice stipulates respect for "Others". By "Others", I mean here other nations and their identities. Global Justice demands that developed countries should give just and fair treamtnet to "Others" who are deprived and underdeveloped. This boils to the point that global justice does not mean equal treatment to all nations. Ordinarily, it is held that global justice contemplates equal treatment to all nations irrespective of race, color and nationality. But I do not subscribe to this principle of equal treatment. This is egalitarian view of global Justice. My submission is that global justice does not mean equal treatment to unequals. Global justice does not afford to give equal treatments to developed, developing and underdeveloped countries. I propose subaltern conception of global justice which is concerned with the upliftment of marginalized nations. India is developing country and it needs more care and aid from developed countries. It is not just to treat developed and underdeveloped countries at par.

Just earlier I have attempted a distinction between egalitarian morality and subaltern morality. Similarly here I conceive two types of global justice: One is egalitarian and other is subaltern. Egalitarian conception of global justice subscribes to the notion of equal treatment to all nations. The other kind of global justice which I propose is "subaltern conception of Global Justice". I adhere that equal treatment to unequals is itself an act of injustice. We can't treat developed and underdeveloped countries equally in matters of awarding grants to developed and underdeveloped nations. As a matter of fact underdeveloped nations deserve more grants than developed nations. Hence I understand that conception of global justice is distributive in nature. Aristotle in his book "Nichomachean Ethics" came up with the suggestion that distributive justice consists of treating equals equally and uneuqals unequally. Distributive justice is based on the principle of equity. There is obvious distinction between equity and equality. The principle of equity is the core element of subaltern global justice. The principle of equality is the basis of egalitarian global justice. Equality is the principle regardless of their inputs. All nations should be given an equal share of the rewards and burden. By global responsibility I mean Nations who have the most should share their resources with those who have less. Global justice is distributive because it conceptualized as fairness associated with outcomes and distribution of resources. By subaltern conception of global justice I mean that those who are marginalized should get fair treatment so that they come in the centre. This subaltern conception of global justice attempts to deconstruct the age-old egalitarian structure of globe by bringing the marginalized nations into the mainstream. The conception of subaltern global justice sounds novel and requires some illustration. The term subaltern was popularized by Italian Marxist philosopher Antonio Gramci. He used it to denote the proletariat class. In the Oxford university some of the historians led by Prof. Ranjit Guha and Gayatri Spivak formed a group of subaltern studies. They started writing history from the viewpoint of common man. Ordinarily history is written about the life and achievements of kings and queens and ordinary man is put on the margin. Actually this term subaltern was popularized by Gramci to counter the ideology of fascism. But I am not a Marxist. I donot subscribe to the view that subaltern can be used in place of proletariat. Proletariate is the economic category whereas subaltern is cultural category. Bu I have taken this from Aristotelian Logic. Hence I take it as logical category applied in social and cultural situations. In Aristotelian logic this term has been used to explain the relationship between two propositions.

He used this terminology to explain the relationship of opposition of propositions. Aristotle used the term subaltern to demonstrate the logical relationship between two propositions having the same subject and predicate but differing in quantity. I found that subaltern group of history writers are oblivious of the logical implications and its application in the field of social and political philosophy. I tried to apply this relation of opposition of propositions in the field of social relationship and proposed subaltern view of morality which stipulates that morality of marginalized people is different from the morality of elite and egalitarian society. In this backdrop I propose "Subaltern Conception of Global justice" which urges that it is the responsibility and moral obligation of developed nations to ameliorate the condition of underdeveloped nations. Global justice demands that backward nations should be uplifted and developed. The inequality prevailing in global society should be lessened. In 2005 & 2007 I visited U.K. and got a chance to travel by train to Edinburg. I saw everywhere written on the walls that "poverty is history". Peter Singer in his book "One World". Observes, "... even if there were no altruistic concern among the rich nations to help the world's poor, their own self-interest should lead them to do so."[6] In the global village other's poverty becomes one's own problem. One of the most influential philosopher like Peter Singer considers ethical issues surrounding globalization. Michael Walzer observes on the back of the book that many people have written about the economic meaning of globalization. In 'One World' Peter Singer explains its moral meaning. Peter Singer shows how global ethic rather than a nationalistic approach can provide answers to global problems. My contention is different from Peter Singer. I contend that national identity and global justice are not mutually exclusive. The subaltern conception of global justice does not counter to national identity. I hold that national identity and the concept of global justice are not logically incompatible. National identity is the primary focus of political legitimacy and the pursuit of justice. To me national identity is a fact. The concept of global justice is not very clear. I understand the concept of global justice is not concerned to war crimes but with socio-economic justice. Here I have concentrated on two focal issues of traditional political philosophy. One is the relation between justice and national identity and the other is scope and limits of equality as a demand of justice. Both are of crucial importance in determining whether we can even form an ideal conception of global justice. The issue of justice presumes sovereignty. National identity comprises two most important components: one is sovereignty and another is cultural values. According to Hobbes sovereignty is essential component of national identity. Hobbes argues that although we can discover the true principles of justice by moral reasoning alone, but actual justice cannot be achieved except sovereign of nation. Justice is the property of the relations among human beings. The liberal requirements of global justice include a strong component of equality among nations. This is a specifically political demand which applies to the basic structure of a global society.

The hallmarks of egalitarian justice are rights and equal opportunity to all. It seems very difficult to resist Hobbe's claim about the relation between justice and sovereignty. I think that sovereignty is an important component of national identity. Broadly speaking we can understand two aspects of the structure of global society. The basic structure consists of sovereignty and super structure consists of cultural values. Hobbes construed the principles of justice as a set of rules and practices that would serve the interest of everyone. The collective self-interest cannot be realised by the independent motivation of self-interested individuals unless each of them has the assurance that others will conform if he does. That assurance requires the external incentive provided by the national identity. But the same need of assurance is present if one construed the principles of justice differently, and attributes to Nations a non-self-interested motive that leads them to want to live on fair terms of some kind with other nations. Even if justice is taken to include not only collective self-interest but also the elimination of morally arbitrary inequalities. I believe that the situation is structurally not very different for conception of global justice that are much more based on the conception of "Others". The conception of global justice without moral base may fall flat. The global justice without sovereignty as stipulated by Hobbes has no practical expressions. If we think from moral perspective then absence of global sovereignty is not a serious obstacle to the concept of global justice. But we have to accept the national identities of "Others" and then we can think of co-operation and moral assurance to maintain moral relations among the citizens of globe. We may reject the Hobbesian contention that justice is the collective self-interest. It is true that for most of us, the ideal of global justice stems from moral motives that cannot be entirely reduced to self-interest. Global conception of justice includes much more than a condition of legally enforced peace and security among interacting nations.

The inequality in the world economy is obvious. Roughly twenty percent people of the globe live on less than a dollar a day. This situation is changing and productivity growth speeds up. Inequality prevailing in the global scenario is so grim that global justice may be a side issue. There are basic questions as what we should do to fulfill the global justice in the absence of global sovereignty. Global justice requires more than mere humanitarian assistance to those who are deprived and marginalized and in desperate need. This is a fact that injustice can persist. Humanitarian duties hold in virtue of the absolute rather than relative level of needs of people. Developed nations are in a position to help underdeveloped nations. Justice is concerned with the relations between the conditions of different classes of people and the causes of inequality between them. The question arises as to how to respond to inequality in general from the point of view of global justice. Postmodern conception of global justice imposes some limitations on the powers of sovereignty. Justice demands fairness or equality of opportunity from the practices that govern our relations with "others". By 'others' I mean national identities of other nations. Global justice is concerned with the relations between the conditions of different nations. The question of global justice will depend on moral conceptions of the relations. There is always possibility of clashes between national identities. There is nothing like global sovereignty to deal with global problems.

The egalitarian conception of justice contemplates equal concern to all. We have to live with just terms with each others who are fellow members of the globe. Equalitarians think that this moral principle of equal treatment apply in principle to all our relations to all "others" not just to our fellow citizens. If we take egalitarian conception of global justice then separate national identities pose obstacle to the establishment or even the pursuit of global justice. But it would be morally inconsistent not to wish, for the world as a whole, a common system of institution that could attempt to realize the same standards of fairness or equal opportunity that one wants for one's own nation. Egalitarian Justice can be realized in a federal system in which members of different nations had special responsibility towards one another. But that would be legitimate only against the background of a global system. At present we do not have any full proof system to legislate justice and injustice in the world. The powerful nations cannot work because they protect their own interest. So the global justice in a sense will be the justice to safeguard the interest of the stronger. Naturally the quest of dominance in the words of Noam Chomsky will mar the sense of global justice. During my stay in Pittsburg I was reading the book entitled "Hegemony or Survival" by Noam Chomsky. On the very first page Chomsky mentions that American's quest for global dominance is apparent, so naturally global justice cannot have hidden meaning of global dominance. Naturally, global justice is subaltern global justice and not a kind of global dominance.

The egalitarian justice suffers from the defects because to treat unequals equally is against the principle of global justice. The conception of global justice which I call as subaltern conception of global justice is concerned with wellbeing of marginalized nations. This conception is exemplified by John Rawls view that justice is well off of the worst off. This conception is concerned with socio-economic situation of the globe. The subaltern conception of global justice presumes the national identities of all nations cannot be effaced. It is not plausible to do away with national identities. Nations do not lose their sovereignty. Every nations has the boundaries and population. It exercises its sovereign power over its citizens. Citizens have responsibilities towards others. The responsibility is sui generics. The obligation of justice and responsibility arise as a result of special relations. The subaltern conception of global justice does not stipulate equal treatment to unequals. The developed and the underdeveloped cannot be treated equally. Hence, the subaltern conception of global justice is distributive in nature. John Rawls insists that different principles apply to different situations. John Rawls observes, "...the correct regulative principle for a thing depends on the nature of that thing"[7] In global justice we contend that nations are free to preserve their national identities. In global context we have to maintain mutual respect and equality of status among nations. This is more difficult than the traditional Hobbesian privileges of sovereignty on the world stage. The responsibility and duties governing relations among nations include, according to John Rawls, not only non-aggression and fidelity to treaties, but also some development assistance to "peoples living under unfavourable conditions that prevent their having a just or decent political and social regime".[8] The consequence seems that if one wants to avoid moral inconsistencies and is favourable to subaltern conception of global justice then one should favour a global difference principle. Moral consistency requires taking nation as the moral units in a conception of global justice. There is no logical or moral inconsistency in accepting national identity as moral unit in global justice. The way to resist egalitarian theory of global justice would deny that there is a universal principle of equal concern, equal status and equal opportunities. The subaltern conception of global justice objects the arbitrary inequalities. National identity gives entitlement to be just and maintain the integrity of the nation but only on the condition that we must learn to respect 'others identities.' Mere economic interaction at global level does not trigger the heightened standard of global justice. There is nothing like global sovereignty at present. There is nothing like global identity. The global identity is dependent on national identity. There are a number of less formal structures that are responsible for a great deal of global governance. National institutions are responsible to their own citizens. But global network does not have the similar responsibility of legislating global justice. Global justice is not merely trading on global level. Global justice is not merely pursuit of common aims by unequal partners. Global justice is based on moral persuasion. I think there is a difference between moral obligation however strong it may be and global justice done and implemented with authority. We cannot ignore the practical difficulty to implement the global justice. But we cannot leave this globe at the mercy of the strong and mighty one. Noam Chomsky in his famous book titled "Hegemony or Survival" talks about America's quest for global dominance. We have to think in terms of global justice instead of global dominance in the 21st century. Noam Chomsky conceived globalization as a new face of capitalism. It means that globalization suffers from all the defects of capitalism. I maintain that globalization in itself is not good or bad but it suffers when it bears the face of new capitalism as contemplated by Noam Chomsky. The subaltern conception of global justice seems plausible because it deconstructs grand hegemony of powerful nations. It grants autonomy to national identity and urges to deconstruct the egalitarian conception of global justice which prepares the ground for rich to become richer and poor to become more poor. The marginalized nations should not be spectators but participants in the process of development and global justice.

References:
1. Peter Singer, One World, Yale University Press, 2004, p. 10
2. Thomas, L. Friedman, The World is Flat, Farrar, Strus and Girous, New York, first edition, 2005, p. 5.
3. Samuel, P. Huntington, The Clash of Civilizations And The Remaking Of World Order, Simon, and Schuster, U.K., 2002, p. 21.
4. Peter Singer, One World, Yale University Press, second edition, 2004, p. 8.
5. John Ralws, A Theory Of Justice, Harvard University Press, 1971, Preface, Px1.
6. Peter Singer, One World, Yale University Press, second edition, 2004, p.7.
7. John Rawls, A Theory of Justice, Cambridge, Massachusetts, Harvard University Press, revised edition, 1971, p. 25.
8. John Rawls, The Law of People, Cambridge, Massachusetts; Harvard University Press, 1991, p. 37.

CHAPTER – VIII

NEW SOCIAL ORDER

Values of new social order are related to contemporary society. The meaning and context of contemporary is very wide but the meaning of post-modern society is very clear. Post-modern is the age of technology. Post-modernism deconstructs the system of conventional structure of value. Post-modernism believes in pluralism and relativism. Values according to post-modernism are relative and not absolute. Post-modernism deconstructs absolute values. It deconstructs abstract and universal values. Post-modernism does not subscribe to Kantian categorical imperative. New social order and its values are post-modern. New social order gives emphasis on culture. By culture I mean cultivation of values. Subaltern moral values are concerned with value of those who are on margins.

It is difficult to define post-modernism. It is complex concept. Some of the philosophers are critical to postmodernism. The word is highly used today. It is equally much misused. Its critics define it as a word of rejection. If we disagree with anything and want to reject anything, we can easily call it postmodern. In the eye of traditional Philosophers, postmodernism thus is a cliche which is often used for rejecting anything.

It would be tragic to look at postmodernism in such a way. It is not fair to label it as destructive. It is a philosophical framework which helps us to understand the reality of social phenomena. The enlightenment project combined with modernity gave a sigh of relief to the liberal humanist ideology. But soon it went wrong. The benefits of modernity were mostly cornered by the elites and the high-ups of the society. Modernity in its turn came to oppress the subaltern people and turned it into certain set ways of thought and actions not always in the interest of subaltern. The subaltern morality in the wake of post-modern society stipulates a new social order. This new social order deconstruct the old social structure as well as the modern structure of centrality and universality. The emergence of technology has changed the face of the world. Indian society has undergone a lot of changes. Throughout the book post-modern vision has been highlighted. On the one hand it deconstructs age-old value systems which are not relevant to-day; on the other hand it also differs from modernity. The new social order does not believe in centrality and excessive rationality. It goes deep in the roots of human life and tradition. It is not cut off from tradition. It understands and interprets tradition in the backdrop of technological advancement. We cannot do away with post-modernity. It is not a myth but reality. Life is deeply concerned with all these hard realities.

In India, modernity has been hijacked by elite classes. The upper caste Hindus and the elite politicians took all the benefits of modernism and technological development. The lower castes, tribals and subaltern groups are nowhere in sight. To combat the challenges of the subaltern of people, modernity has in a sophisticated way created meta-narratives as coined by Jean-Francois Lyotard. These meta or grand narratives have been established as universalizing values. Marxism, democracy and capitalism are glaring examples of grand narratives created by modernity to defeat the cause of subalterns who are characterized by 'culture of silence and just standing on margins'.

The grand narratives have also given fundamentalism reasserting itself. There is eco-fundamentalism, academic fundamentalism and in the economic realm, there is market fundamentalism. Wherever we see in this country, modernity has created grand narratives of values. Post-modernism attempts to deconstruct the grand narratives of value system. Post-modernism believes in multi narratives and pluralism.

Postmodernity has a colossal task to perform. Institutional authority like religious, educational, economic and developmental are required to be deconstructed by the postmodernity. Post-modernity puts a challenge to modernity. It looks with skepticism all the vague notions of progress. It argues for the rejection of universalistic beliefs and abstract truths.

Philosophy is not speculative. The post-modernism leans towards functionalism. The functionalism is charged with empiricism. It has played a dismal role in philosophizing. The perspectives of functionalism, which have been applied in the study of caste, class, family, village and tribals in Indian society, have given us a distorted image of Indian society. We are put to a land which is embedded with status quo. It subscribes to conservatism. The applied philosophy 'educate' us that there is subtle change occurring in Indian society. We speak of change but in reality there is no change.

Critics may say it is all a gimmick or verbose. But I think philosophizing in India is also taking a new dimension. Classical way of philosophizing tends to create a system. It loved system building. But new way of philosophizing is relating one concept to the other.

In the present chapter I have applied the perspectives of postmodernism to analyze the concept of subaltern morality. Indian society is increasingly becoming postmodern. Subaltern morality is a new concept emerging in post-modern society. To me, postmodernity tries to understand the nature of contemporary man. The contemporary society suffers from inconsistencies and contradictions. The concept of modernity in these countries is outdated. But no philosophy today is complete without a debate on postmodernity.

Contemporary Indian Philosophers like Sri Aurobindo and Radhakrishnan write on our traditional themes of family, caste, kinship, marriage, religion and village communities. Most of the Indian philosophers are no ordinary celebrities. They have argued that we have been mistaken about 'modernity'. In fact, we are far away from modernity. Modernity is an incomplete project in India. But due to technological development post-modernity emerged.

The application of philosophical principles in life situation is the present day trends of philosophy. It is the guiding paradigm of Indian philosophy. Modern India does not negate world. Indian philosophy is life affirming and not life negating as contemplated by Albert Schweitzer. Take for instance the philosophy of Bhagwat Gita. This depicts the whole concept of life during the course of war. Bhagavad Gita is a part of the Great Mahabharat which depicts the fierce war between Kaurav and Pandav. They constantly argue that Indian society is in a process of rapid transformation. For Indians, the massive change is 'adaptive change'. The argument is something like this: there are traditions in India which have not been changed, they still maintain their status quo; at the most they have been partly modernized. This is how functionalism has put Indian philosophy of value as dynamic and not static.

Elite castes behavior and value systems are the imitation models for the subaltern people. My conception of subaltern is different from proletariat. Ordinarily by subaltern, we mean proletariat. But by subaltern I do not understand as proletariat class. Subaltern is cultural category I understand it as inclusive concept. In this process of the so-called cultural change there is no question for the loss of identity of subaltern. They undergo improvement. The gap between elite and subaltern is minimised.

The concept of sanskritization was proposed by M.N. Srinivas a noted sociologist of India to describe the process of social change and emergence of new social order. The term used at first was Brahmanization. Later on the expression 'Sanskritisation' was in vogue. Such a contribution by an eminent thinker was given to the succeeding generation with the hope that the subaltern would transform themselves on the lines or model of the higher and dominant caste. What would be the effect of this process on the subaltern people? The knowledge of these processes of cultural changes is always and invariably in the form of the courses on sanskritization and its allied processes.

The structure of society that India had during the epic period of India does not exist today. Our civilization was great indeed. But some of traditional values have outlived its utility. How can and do we justify our contemporary existence by clinging to the concepts of glorified joint family, caste and panch parmeshwar? Our perspectives of understanding and analyzing society are merely mythological. It requires to be understood in modern perspective. We can deconstruct old values and create some new values. The new social order cannot adhere some of the outdated and old values.

Some philosophers in our country have shown fondness for ethnicity and modernity. First, it was the turn of ethnicity. Our anthropological literature is very rich in ethnicity. We have made fantastic claims on the achievements of our village communities. Modernity went a step further. It made attempts to give a death blow to hackneyed tradition. There is a broad consensus among all contemporary philosophers on modernity that it involves a belief in the possibility of human progress. The modern age believes in rationality. Rational planning to achieve its objectives; a belief in the modernity; trusts in the ability of technology and science to solve human problems.

Society developed hand in hand with modernity. Durkheim, Max Weber and Karl Marx tended to believe that societies progress with the progress of technology. Scientific principles would be used to understand society. Rational thought could be employed to ensure that society was so organized as to fulfil and meet human needs. About two hundred years have passed since the working of the process of modernization in India. But nothing substantial has happened. It has been difficult to get out of the rut of some of old values. But winds of change have begun to blow.

Philosophers took up the theme of modernity sometimes in the beginning of seventies. But, the perspectives adopted by them were erroneous. We can't discuss the issue of Indian modernity in the idioms of western terminology. It is also true that we cannot analyze Indian modernity only in the context of India's tradition. For philosophers traditions mean hierarchy, holism, continuity and transcendence. I think modernity is not break from tradition. It absorbs the essence of tradition and continues. Indian Philosophers make straightjacket classification of Western and Indian societies. The former being egalitarian and the latter hierarchical. In other words, Indian society is a traditional society and the western society a modern one. Contemporary Indian thinkers are so much obsessed by the civilizational depth of India that they conclude by saying that a strange kind of adaptive transformation is taking place in India which makes traditions to take on modernity. Obviously, the present day society is very much influenced by India's civilizations and British inspired functionalism.

Modernism failed in the west. The euphoria of enlightenment and modernity has left people disenchanted. The philosophers of these countries moved along with the times more or less, abandoning modernity. The west has ceased to be the centre of social inspiration. Danial Bell's famous volume, "The Cultural Contradictions of Capitalism (1976)", has presented a poignant diagnosis of ailing segments of American society. He demonstrated the dissociation of norms from values and of means from ends. Daniel Bell says that modernity in its post-war phase, suffered a credibility crisis. This crisis made suspect the ruling assumption of modernity, namely, the assumption that science, reason, and rationality would lead to the making and shaping of a sane and sensible society.

The new social order does focus on the transformation resulting from it which has been analyzed only as adaptive culture change. The social structure in this process does not experience any radical change. It retains its identity, content and structure. The changes are only superficial displaying a modern facility. Tradition, civilization, culture and norms are intact in the Indian model of modernity. So there is not a break from old values as we find in the west. There is sense in continuity of values. We can extend the same logic from modernity to post-modernity. There is certainly a transition. Postmodernity symbolizes both a critique of modernity as well as a new appreciation of the current nature of social processes and the consequent emergence of a new conception of social order.

Those of the contemporary philosophy who have analyzed the impact of modernity invariably talk about tradition. Term 'tradition' is used with reference to civilization. The whole treatment of civilization is in the terms of Samuel Huntington's influential book, "The Clash of Civilizations and the Remaking of the World Order" The difficulty with Huntington is that he classifies civilizations largely on the basis of religion. He contrasts civilizations as 'Islamic civilziation', 'Hindu civilization', 'Buddhist civilization' and so on. We explain modernity in terms of tradition. Modernity and post-modernity are not a break from Hindu civilizations. Hierarchy, holism, continuity and transcendence are all important factors of Hindu mythology. The Indian view on modernity is essentially civilizational.

The word 'tradition' connotes the act of handing down a set of values from one generation to another. A civilization may be thought of then as a structure of tradition. It is a form of arrangements for the handing down of cultural substance within a great community. The local community within a civilization is ideationally, intellectually, and often morally, 'heteronomous' - dependent on norms coming to it from without. If we carefully analyze the essays contained in Milton Singer's edited volume, "Traditional India (1975)", we will find that it is Hindu India to the exclusion of Muslims, Christians and Jews. India's traditions, such as, hierarchy, caste, holism, continuity and transcendence, are in a state of adaptive transformation and are getting modern. He also wants to convey that Hindu civilization is getting modernized. He has, however, a soft corner for Islam and modernization in India. But he does not take into account other ethnic groups of the country such as Sikh, Jain and Buddhist.

The civilizational approach taken by social philosophers and anthropologists in the study and analysis of the impact of modernization in India is obviously sectarian and biased. Civilization has continuity. It carries with it an organization of traditions. But it is not always that civilization and for that matter, traditions are not without diversity. Amartya Sen, in his book entitled "Identity and Violence" while rejecting Samuel Huntington's thesis of civilizational clash he observes that civilizational clash suffers from foggy perception of world history which overlooks, first, the extent of internal diversities within these civilizational categories, and second, the reach and influence of interactions - intellectual as well as material- that go right across the regional borders of so-called civilizations.

The applied philosophers forget that the impact of modernization is not similar on all the traditions. To consider modernity with tradition is theoretically wrong. If we look at the Indian experience of modernity, the fallout is not satisfactory. Our expectation with the modernity was that it will provide us all-round development. Our villages will get self-sufficiency. Agriculture would enable the people to fulfil their livelihood needs. It was believed that green revolution would strengthen the poor peasant. But modernization did not bring any worthwhile change in the poor status of the farmers. At the urban level, the general masses are alienated. Similar is the output of our democracy. Adaptive transformation experienced in the wake of modernization has made Indian society a victim of pessimism.

Recently India has shun the attitude of pessimism and in the field of computer science it has made a remarkable development. It was due to modernity that the subaltern people suffered. Social stratification became sharp. Caste and religious identities took the shape of fundamentalism. The ethnic elaboration which social philosophers made in their works proved to be harmful to the Indian social order. Modernity, democracy and capitalism worsened the already deteriorating status of the subalterns.

It appears that modernity has failed as a process of transformation or there are changes which have benefited only the higher castes and elites. Postmodernity has thrown a challenge to modernity. It was expected that with the coming of modernity, Indian society, mainly its subalterns, would come out of the rut and make progress. History would be forward looking. But it did not happen.

Why is it that despite social policy to bring about change, the norms of social hierarchy, degree of empowerment of women and extent of religious and cultural tolerance remain confounded? Culture changes only slowly and adaptively, social philosophers have variously explained it as being a result of the fact that a culture is always interactively continued. Each culture has a basic 'theme' or 'pattern' or 'symbolic code' which constitutes its core, and all changes in it are mediated by it.

The Indian society has been suffering terribly. Democracy has been abused. Economic growth has gone in favour of the rich. People have lost faith in science and technology. They have become aware of damaging effects of pollution, the dangers of a future nuclear war and risks of genetic enginnering. People have become more sceptical about the benefits of rational planning. As a matter of fact, people have lost faith in the loudly proclaimed public policy and grand legislation that claim to be able to improve the lot of marginalised people of society. It has been a common observation in India that only modernity-inspired rationalism cannot solve the manifold complex problems of the subaltern. The advocates of the idea of postmodernism claim that the classic social thinkers took their inspiration from the idea that history has a shape. It goes somewhere and leads to progress. This notion has collapsed. There are no longer any 'grand narratives' or 'meta narratives'. There is no general notion of progress that can be defended. There is no such thing as history itself.

Indian social philosophers have created a huge literature on caste system. Castes are the oldest social formations of Indian society. These hierarchy-based divisions have not posed any challenge to the society. They were considered to be a part of our all-enveloping religion. There are ample evidences to prove that Indian society was essentially a caste-based society. But, with the coming of modernity to India, the society developed a caste identity. There has been a vigorous development of caste consciousness, which is called casteism. Politics plays a dangerous role to benefit from caste identity. This identity has many faces. It also has a role to play in voting behaviour, economic development and social change. Amartya Sen upholds that most of current fire of India is due to the conflicting identities of the people-religiously and linguistically divided. Amartya Sen diagnoses the structure of identity and says that a person has multiple identities. When philosophers argue that caste identity is culture identity, they are mostly mistaken. When S.C. Dube tried to measure the impact of community development, he did so by taking Rajput village and other caste villages in his book India's Changing Villages. To him caste is a major determinant of development. The tendency of social philosophers has been to assess secular themes in the perspective of culture and culture for them has always been religion, caste and fundamentalism. Amartya Sen is very specific when he clarifies the concept of identity:

Our cultural identities can be extremely important. Identities do not stand above and aloof from other influences on our understanding and priorities. There are a number of qualifications that have to make while acknowledging the influence of culture on human lives and actions. First, important as culture is, it is not uniquely significant in determining our lives and identities. Other things, such as class, race, gender, profession, politics, also matter, and can matter powerfully. Culture is not homogenous attribution. There can be great variations even within the same general cultural milieu. Culture interacts with other determinants of social perception and action. For example, economic globalization brings in not only more trade, but also more global music and cinema. Culture cannot be seen as an isolated force independent of other influences. The presumption of individuality can be deeply ignored.

Here I have tried to explain that philosophy is an intellectual discourse. Philosophers have certain obligations towards the society. In the past, the mainstream philosophy has not done anything worthwhile for the improvement of Indian society. Its methodology - functionalism - has always remained conservative. In the name of culture and cultural transformation, it has always talked about adaptive pattern of change. The western approach has been straight forward. When philosophers found that Durkheim, Max Weber and Karl Marx - ceased to have their relevance in a fast changing world, Talcott Parsons, Robert Merton, Peter Balau- have also been questioned. Hardly anyone cares to read them. They have lost their relevance in the attempts to solve the problems of their society. Now, they are trying postmodern thinkers. Philosophers express their disenchantment with the outcome of the process of modernization. They argue that the contemporary western countries are constantly in state of flux.

Our Indian society is being remade. In recent years the buzz word is development. Mass production, the mass consumer, the big city, big brother state, the sprawling housing estate, and the nation-state are in decline; flexibility, diversity, differentiation, mobility, communication, decentralization, and internationalization are in the ascendance. In the process, our own identities, our sense of self, our own subjectivities are being transformed. We are in transition to a new social order. The new social order constructs new moral values. Life of marginalized people are changing due to technological advancement. In global scenario technological knowledge shapes the society. Caste systems are not prevalent in the metro cities of India.

The modernity which India witnessed during the last about two hundred years has been a study of society as a whole. The modern perspective has not succeeded in understanding the reality of our society. As a consequence of it, postmodernity has taken over. Society is now seen as a reality too devoid of centrally binding and cohering entity to be conceived of as a totality. I do not argue that postmodernity will solve our problems. Post-modern age has put challenges to our society. The conventional paradigm as characterized by historicism, functionalism, totalitariansim are under circle. We are bound to create a new social order. This new social order will give rise to new morality. Technology is fast moving and society cannot go back to machine age. Post-modern age is the age of technology. Technology has effaced many old identities and created a new identities. In India society is moving fast due to tremendous technological improvement.

CONCLUSION

I propose the concept of subaltern morality in the backdrop of Aristotelian logic. The subaltern studies had published several volumes on South Asian History and Society from a subaltern perspective. They have attempted to rectify the elitist bias in history writings. The contribution related to history, politics, economics and sociology are remarkable. But I have tried to streamline subaltern morality and not subaltern history. My approach is quite different. The subaltern morality attempts to deconstruct the age-old value system. Keeping in view the process of change and social mobility, subaltern people are in process of deconstructing traditional values and social structures. It is true that subaltern morality emerges in the post-modern society. There are two types of morality, the one is egalitarian and the other is subaltern. The marginalised people show scant respect for traditional values. It may take years to deconstruct the value system of egalitarian morality. But those who are on the margins are trying to deconstruct the old narratives.

In the first chapter I have tried to give an introduction to the concept of subaltern morality. In the second chapter I have outline the nature and meaning of "Applied Ethics" in post-modern background. In applied ethics, the ethical principles are required to be applied to solve the riddles of life. In the concept of subaltern morality the situation is important. I contend that subaltern morality is new trend in applied ethics. Applied ethics provides frameworks within which practical moral problems can be solved. In the twentieth century philosophers were engaged in linguistic analysis. After 1980, philosophizing is no more simply conceptual analysis. In the twentieth century, philosophizing is conceptualising. Concepts are clothe in language. Thus linguistic analysis was very much current. I have not attempted to separate theoretical ethics and applied ethics. There is need to integrate theory and practice. Subaltern morality deconstructs grand narratives and subscribes to multi-narratives. Ethics is not universalistic in nature. It is relative to human situation and values. In the third chapter, I have attempted to streamline the nature and meaning of social development. I contend that subaltern morality and its value systems emerge in the course of historical process. By development I mean total development of human existence. This is inclusive concept which integrates both economic and cultural aspects of life and society. Historical process has been conceived in two ways. One is idealistic; another is materialistic. Hegel is the champion of idealistic dialectic process and Marx is upholder of materialistic dialectic process. The meaning of history has been conceived as process. The meaning of history has not been confined to the stories and struggle of kings and kingdoms. It is not simply story of events. Francis Fukuyama has written a book entitled "The End of History and The Last Man". It stipulates that liberal democracy has won. The end of history means the end of dialectical process as conceived by Marx. The victory of liberal democracy presupposes the end of communism and rise of nationalism. Nationalism is a great value. Nationalism is opposed to internationalism. Amartya Sen in his book "Identity and Violence" upholds that identity causes violence. He is not in favour of national identity or nationalism. Tolstoy in his book "War and Peace" suggests that nationalism is the cause of war. Both are against national identity and values attached to identity. Here I donot subscribe to views of Tolstoy and Amartya Sen. My argument is that to say that one should shun national identity is to say that one should jump out of his body. This is not possible to skip out of his own body. Hence I think that contention of Tolstoy and Amartya Sen is abstract. It is not plausible to get rid of national identity. Gandhi in his book "Hindswaraj" has emphasized that the feeling of nationalism is not the potential cause of struggle and clash between two nations. It is our attitude which causes clashes. Post-modernism believes that class struggle is over with the rise of globalisation and liberal democracy. In the history of world process, the class struggle is no more effective. In post-modern age technology has developed and it has influenced the deep rooted traditional problems. The new social order will be shaped by technology.

The fourth chapter deals with social progress and emergence of subaltern morality. Here subaltern morality has been discussed in the light of Shankara's book entitled "Manisha Panchkam". The argument in favour of equality has been advanced within the framework of Vedantic Logic that the same soul persists in each and every being. The caste discrimination is not appreciated in Advaitism. Social progress is through conflicts. The moral development presupposes conflicts. In hierarchical Indian society caste conflicts are reality. The subaltern morality contemplates that the traditional value system requires to be reformulated in the wake of technological advancement. Philosophical deliberations give way to new ethics. This new ethics will create new value system primarily keeping in view of the subaltern.

In the fifth chapter we consider subaltern narratives in the light of views of Gandhi and Ambedkar. Subaltern narrative streamlines the discrimination done to them in the historical process of social development. The identity of schedule caste and schedule tribe is linked with poverty. Schedule castes are marginalised even if they are economically well off they are put under the category of subaltern because of their cultural marginalisation. Subaltern narratives cannot be confined to economic discourse. Marxism and Gandhi have different perspectives towards the problem of subaltern. The demand of subaltern is related to their identity and dignity. Dalits are on the margins not only on the grounds of economics but they are being dubbed as 'untouchables'. My approach to subaltern morality is different from Marxist approach. I contend that it is wrong notion that Marxist alone can talk about subaltern and poverty.

The sixth chapter has dealt with subaltern morality in Post-Ramayana Ramkatha. Here I have made an attempt to emphasise subaltern ethical problems spread in some versions of Post-Ramayan Ramkatha. Ramayana has produced profound influence on the life of people. It portrays human drama and moral conflicts. The treatment of subaltern in the Ramcharitramanas raises some ethical questions. In ancient and medieval time the attitudes were not favourable towards subaltern people. Subaltern morality is concerned with the justice of subordinate Nisad and Sabari of Ramkatha. The marginalised dalits were brought to centre. The subaltern can be termed as the 'other'. B.R. Ambedkar charged that the Ramcharitramans is against shudra. As regards the summary execution of the ascetic Shambuka the alleged action of Rama has been criticised by Ambedkar. Ram was advised by seers to follow Rajdharma. There was a conflict between Rajdharma and feeling of pity towards Shambuka. Valmiki Ramayana could not justify this event. Nisad, Kevat and Sabri are witness to Rama's attitude towards subaltern as class. Tulsi does not look down upon subaltern as class. If there was conflict between Rajdharma and caste consideration during epic period, Rajdharma will override caste consideration. However, this point requires a fresh thinking in Post-Ramayana Ramkatha literature.

The seventh chapter is entitled "Global Justice". Here I contend that global justice is based on Aristotelian conception of distributive justice. Aristotle's theory of justice is distributive in nature. Justice is concerned with treating equals equally and unequals unequally. It is not just to treat healthy person and diabetic one equally while distributing food and medicine. I think globalization as a process of development is just but as an instrument of exploitation is unjust. Globalization is faced with a paradox. If we go against globalization, then we will be technologically backward to be poor and underdeveloped. The backwardness will cause poverty. In order to get rid of poverty we have to accept technology. It has changed everything. Wanton use of technology is not good. Sustainable development is desirable. Thomas Friedman in his book "The World is Flat" has conceived that world has become flat. Professor

Huntington in his book "The Clash of Civilization and the Remaking of World Order" upholds that global politics is multi-civilizational. The most important distinction is not economic but cultural. Global justice stipulates respect for 'others'. By 'others', I mean other nations and their identities. The concept of global justice demands that developed countries should give fair treatment to 'others'. Aristotle in his book "Nichomachean Ethics" came with the suggestion that distributive justice consists of treating equals equally and unequal's unequally. Distributive justice is based on the principle of equity. The principle of equity is the core of subaltern global justice. The quest of dominance in the words of Noam Chomsky will mar the sense of global justice. Noam Chomsky conceived globalization as a new doctrine of dominance in the 21st century. Noam Chomsky conceived globalization as a new form of capitalism. The subaltern conception of global justice seems plausible because it deconstructs grand hegemony of powerful nations.

The eighth chapter is captioned as "New Social Order". It has been contemplated that a new trend is emerging in contemporary Indian society. Post-modernism is not a sudden break from tradition. It is trying to go back to tradition. Modernism was against tradition but post-modernism absorbs the essence of tradition and modernity and creates a new value system. Some of Indian philosophers are critical to post-modernism. Its critics define it as a word of rejection. The expression post-modernism is viewed with reproach. If we want to reject anything, we call it post-modern. It is often used for rejecting anything. Post-modernity puts a challenge to abstract thought but it is comfortable with traditional roots. The applied philosophy educates us that there is subtle change occurring in Indian society. Philosophizing in India is taking a new dimension. The development through sanskritization has changed the structure of society. Indian social structure is not static but dynamic. The caste system is also not fixed but dynamic. Structural caste system as envisaged in the Purush Shukta has been changed as functional one in Buddhist period. The Indian philosophy is tradition bound but it is dynamic. The new technology is shaping the society and values of life. Though the Indian society retains its cultural identity yet it deconstructs some of the old values of life. It appears that modernity has failed as a process of transformation. It has benefitted only the higher castes and elites. Post modernity has thrown a challenge to modernity. The new social order constructs new moral values. In global scenario technology shapes our values and life. In this changing scenario in the wake of technological advancement and globalization hierarchical caste system is melting. The new value systems are emerging in post-modern society. This prompted me to propose and develop subaltern morality.

BIBLIOGRAPHY

Adorno, Theador, Negative Dialectics, Continuum, New York, 1973.

A.J. Ayer; Language, Truth and Logic, Penguin Books, England, 1980.

Amartya Sen; Identity and Violence. Allen & Unwin Penguin Books, 2006.

Antonio Gramsci; Selection from the Prison Notebook, Lawrence and Wishart, 1971.

Arendt, Hannah, The Human Condition, University of Chicago Press, 1958.

Appiah, Kwame Anthony, Cosmopolitanism: Ethics in a World of Strangers. Issues of Our Times Series, New York, 2006.

____. The Ethics of Identity, Princeton University Press, New Jersey, U.S.A., 2007.

____. In My Father's House: Africa in the Philosophy of Culture, New York: Oxford University Press, 1993.

Barry, Christian, and Thomas W. Pogge, eds. Global Institutions and Responsibilities: Achieving Global Justice. Metaphilosophy Series, Malden, MA: Blackwell/Wiley, 2005.

Bertrand Russell,; Education and Social Order, Allen & Unwin, 1932.

____; Human Society in Ethics and Politics, Allen & Unwin, 1954.

____; Mysticism and Logic, Allen and Unwin, Second edition, 1929.

____; An Enquiry into Meaning and Truth, Allen and Unwin, 1940.

____; Marriage and Morals, Allen & Unwin, 1929.

Bernard Williams, Ethics and the Limits of Philosophy, Harvard University Press, 1985.

Carr, E.H. What is History? Penguin, London, 2008.

C.L. Stevension; Ethics and Language, Yale University Press, 1965.

Charles Taylor, The Ethics of Authenticity, Harvard University Press, 1997.

Coetzee, P.H., and A.P.J.Roux, eds. The African Philosophy Reader. Second Edition, Routledge, 1998, 2003.

Crocker, David A. Ethics of Global Development: Agency,Capability, and Deliberative Democracy, Cambridge University Press, New York, 2008.

David Ludden (ed.); Reading Subaltern Studies, Permanent black, Third impression, 2008.

Dall Mayr, Fred. Alternate Visions: Paths in the Global Village. Philosophy and Global Context Series. Lanham, MD: Rowman and Littlefield, 1998.

D.D. Raphel; Moral Philosophy, Oxford University Press, 1981.

Deutsch, Eliot. Persons and Valuable Worlds. Philososphy and Global Context Series. Lanham, MD: Rowman and Littlefield, 2002.

Dipesh Chakrabarty, Marx after Marxism; Subaltern Histories and the Question of Difference in Polygraph, 1993.

Dummet, Michael. On Immigration and Refugees. Thinking in Action Series. Routledge, New York, 2001.

Emile Durkheim, The Rules of Sociological Method, Free Press, Chicago, 1950.

Eze, Emmanuel Chukwudi, ed. African Philosophy: An Anthology. Malden, MA: Wiley-Blackwell, 1998.

____, ed. Postcolonial African Philospher: A Critical Reader, Critical Readers Series, 1997. Malden, MA: Wiley-Blackwell, 1997.

____, ed. Race and the Enlightenment: A Reader, Malden, MA: Wiley-Blackwell, 2008.

Francis Fukuyama; The End of Order, The Social Market Foundation, London, 1967.

Ganeri, Jonardan (ed); The Collected Essays of Bimal Krishna Matilal; Ethics and Epics, Oxford University Press, New Delhi, 2002

Guha, Ramachandra, Environmentalism; A Global History, Oxford University Press, New Delhi, 2000.

Guha, Ramchandra (ed) Subaltern Studies, Oxford University Press, Published in India, 1982.

Goldstein, Fred. Low Wage Capitalism: Colossus with Feet of Clay — What the New Globalized, High-Tech Imperialism Means for the Class Struggle in the US. New York: World View Forum, 2008.

Gosselin, Abigail, Global Poverty and Individual Responsibility. Lanham, MD: Lexington Books, Rowman and Littlefield, 2008.

Gupta, Bina, Ethical Questions: East and West. Philosophy and Global Context Series. Lanham, MD: Rowman and Littlefield, 2002.

___, and J.N. Mohanty, eds. Philosophy Questions: East and West. Philosophy and Global Context Series. Lanham, MD: Rowman and Littlefield, 2000.

Hindery, Roderick; Comparative Ethics in Hindu and Buddhist Traditions, Motilal Banarasidas, Delhi, 1978.

Iris Marion Young, Justice and the Politics of Difference, Princeton University Press, New Jersy, 2011.

Jurgen Habermas; Moral Consciousness and Communicative Action (Translated by Christian Lenhardt and Shierry Weber Nicholwen) The MIT Press, Cambridge, Massachusetts, 1999.

Jurgen Habermas; Communication and the Evolution of Society, Boston, 1979.

John Rawls, A Theory of Justice, Harvard University Press, Cambridge, 1971.

Karl Mannheim, Ideology and Utopia, Routledge & Kegan Paul, London, 1936.

Kant, Immanuel, Critique of Pure Reason, (ed. and Translated by P. Guyer and A.W. Wood) Cambridge University Press, 1998.

Kymlicka, Will. Multicultural Citizenship: A Liberal Theory of Minority Rights. Oxford Political Theory Series. New York: Oxford University Press, 1996.

Lawson, Bill, E., ed. The Underclass Question, Temple University Press, Philadelphia, 1992.

MacIntyre, Alasdair; A Short History of Ethics, Routledge, London, 2010.

Max Weber; The Theory of Social and Economic Organizations, Oxford University Press, New York, 1947.

____; The Protestant Ethic and the Spirit of Capitalism, Dover Publications, New York, 2003.

Michael, J. Sandel; Justice, Farrar, Straus and Giroux, New York, 2010.

Michael Foucaulte, Ehtics: Subjectivity and Truth, The New Press, New York, 1998.

Moore, G.E., Principia Ethica, Cambridge Press, 1954.

M.V. Nadkarni; Ethics for our Times, Oxford University Press, New Delhi, 2011.

Nirmal Kumar Bose; Problems of National Integration, Indian Institute of Advanced Study, Shimla, 1967.

Nussbaum, Martha, Sex and Social Justice. New York: Oxford University Press, 2004.

____. Women and Human Development: The Capabilities Approach. New York: Cambridge University Press, 2001.

Osborne, Arthur, Ramana Maharshi and the Path of Self-knowledge, Rider, London, 1992.

Okin, Susan Moller. Is Multiculturalism Bad for Women? Edited by Joshua Cohen, Mathew Howard, and Martha C. Nussbaum. Princeton University Press, 1999.

Peter, L. Berger & Thomas Luckman; The Social Construction of Reality, Anchor Books, A division of Random House, New York, 1967.

Popper, Karl; The Open Society and its Enemies, Vol. I & II, Routledg, Kegan Paul Ltd., New York, 2003.

Richard Rorty, Philosophy and the Mirror of Nature, Princeton, 1979.

Sen, Amartya. Identity and Violence: The Illusion of Destiny. Issues of Our Times Series. New York: W.W. Norton, 2006.

Singer, Peter. One World: The Ethics of Globalization, Second edition, Orient Longman, India, 2004.

Sterba, James P., ed. Ethics: Classical Western Texts in Feminist and Multicultural Perspectives. New York: Oxford University Press, 1999.

____. Three Challenges to Ethics: Environmentalism. Feminism, and Multiculturalism. New York: Oxford University Prress, 2000.

Ted Honderich and Myles Burnyeat (ed.) Philosophy As It Is, A Penguin Book, London, 1993.

Walzer, Michael. On Toleration. New Haven, CT: Yale University Press, 1997.

Waters, Anne, ed. American Indian Thought: Philosophical Essays. Malden, MA: Wiley-Blackwell, 2003.

Wilson, Richard A., and Richard D. Brown, eds. Humanitarianism and Suffering: The Mobilization of Empathy, Cambridge University Press, New York, 2008.

Wittgenstein; Ludwig; Notebook 1914-16, Trans. G.E.M. Anscombe, (ed.),G.H. Van Wright and G.E. Anscombe, Oxford, Basil Blackwell, 1961.